HOW TO CREATE YOUR OWN DESIGNS

Also by Dona Z. Meilach

A MODERN APPROACH TO BASKETRY
CONTEMPORARY ART WITH WOOD
CONTEMPORARY BATIK AND TIE-DYE
CONTEMPORARY LEATHER: ART AND ACCESSORIES
CONTEMPORARY STONE SCULPTURE
CREATING ART FROM ANYTHING
CREATING ART FROM FIBERS AND FABRICS
CREATIVE CARVING
CREATING WITH PLASTER
MACRAMÉ ACCESSORIES
MACRAMÉ: CREATIVE DESIGN IN KNOTTING
MAKING CONTEMPORARY RUGS AND WALL HANGINGS
PAPERCRAFT
PAPIER-MÂCHÉ ARTISTRY
PRINTMAKING
SOFT SCULPTURE AND OTHER SOFT ART FORMS
THE ARTIST'S EYE

COLLAGE AND ASSEMBLAGE (with Elvie Ten Hoor)
COLLAGE AND FOUND ART (with Elvie Ten Hoor)
CREATIVE STITCHERY (with Lee Erlin Snow)
WEAVING OFF LOOM (with Lee Erlin Snow)
DIRECT METAL SCULPTURE (with Donald Seiden)
SCULPTURE CASTING (with Dennis Kowal)
ACCENT ON CRAFTS

How to Create

DONA Z. MEILACH JAY HINZ BILL HINZ

Your Own Designs

AN INTRODUCTION TO COLOR, FORM & COMPOSITION

DOUBLEDAY & COMPANY, INC., GARDEN CITY, NEW YORK

Dedicated to Mary and George Stuart

all photographs by Dona Meilach
unless otherwise credited

Library of Congress Cataloging in Publication Data
Meilach, Dona Z
How to create your own designs.
Bibliography: p. 214
1. Handicraft. 2. Design. I. Hinz, Jay, joint
author. II. Hinz, Bill, joint author. III. Title.
TT149.M46 745.5
ISBN 0-385-01877-0
Library of Congress Catalog Card Number 74–130

Printed in the United States of America
9 8 7 6 5 4 3

CONTENTS

ACKNOWLEDGMENTS

Compiling a book such as this relies on the effort and cooperation of so many generous people. We are especially indebted to the artists and craftsmen who created designs especially for the book, and their names are credited where their work is shown.

We are also grateful to those who permitted us to photograph their work and to the artists who took their own photos or had them taken. We appreciate the work of professional photographers whose design concepts in their exacting medium helped bring about the total visual presentation.

We want to thank the many museum curators and gallery directors who supplied photos from their collections.

Dr. Melvin Meilach has our great admiration for his extensive photo collection uniquely aimed at images that stimulate artistic thought. We are grateful to Ben Lavitt and Harold Smolar of Astra Photo Service, Chicago, for their continued excellence in photoprocessing and for their advice on technical problems. We appreciate the efforts of Rita Kappel who typed our final manuscript into the necessary presentable order it required.

Finally, we want to acknowledge that compiling the material and working with the artists, photographers, and scores of other creative people has been a delightful learning process for all of us as we delved into one another's skills, talents, and knowledge.

Dona Z. Meilach
Jay Hinz
Bill Hinz

FOREWORD

Design. What is it? How do you create it? How does one extract what he sees and learn to put it on paper, in a sculpture, on fabric, in ceramics, as jewelry, so that it is pleasing, well ordered, and expressive? What are the secrets of the successful designer?

Actually, there are no secrets about design. It is a study in itself just as any other aspect of a field. Breaking down the concepts of design so that they can be studied, selected, and employed in different media is an exciting and revealing process. The results are well worth the effort involved.

HOW TO CREATE YOUR OWN DESIGNS is aimed at the student, teacher, and everyone whether he works with oil paint, acrylics, clay, yarns, hammered metal, cast metals, fibers, and so forth. It is designed so that the reader can easily grasp the *elements* and the *principles* of design and learn to isolate them, then combine them in any art or craft approach. It is planned to open the reader's eyes to the sources for design that are ever-present and then relate them to his own work. You'll discover the vocabulary used by artists to observe, analyze, sense, and feel what design is and how it is created.

Where are the design stimulae? How do you apply them to your art or craft? These are the questions that are asked and answered throughout the book in abundant copy, photos, and captions. In addition, each chapter provides a problem or series of exercises to jolt your mind into coping with the concepts introduced and applying them to your own creativity.

We feel that HOW TO CREATE YOUR OWN DESIGNS is a practical, workable, and essential approach for everyone interested in any and every aspect of arts and crafts whether they are a student, a teacher, a professional artist, or a collector.

CHAPTER 1

What Is Design ?

Design equals order. Design is the process of organizing space; it is also the product that results from a planned organization. The word design often connotes surface decoration; but in the context of this book it will also encompass the problems of composition and form. Regardless of his media, an artist must respect aspects of design whether he is planning a fabric decoration, a painting, or a sculpture.

To discuss and discover design, including composition and form, a certain vocabulary is necessary with common definitions. The mathematician devised a language to explain geometric forms: squares, rectangles, triangles, circles; the artist refers to *elements* and *principles*.

The *elements* and *principles* must be singled out, defined, and studied, so that the artist or craftsman can consciously select one or more of them to combine in any object he creates.

The *elements* consist of *dot, line, shape, texture, value,* and *color*.

Each **element** of design must be considered separately as a building unit. Each will be analyzed to promote a thorough awareness and understanding of its peculiar role within the structure of a total design. Several elements usually exist simultaneously within a design; this overlapping can make it difficult to isolate one from another for identification and examination.

If the *elements* are the building blocks, then the **principles** may be considered the binders that cement the building blocks together and in place.

Roottree. Jay Hinz. 1973. 10¼″ high, 7″ wide. Ink drawing, negative photostat.

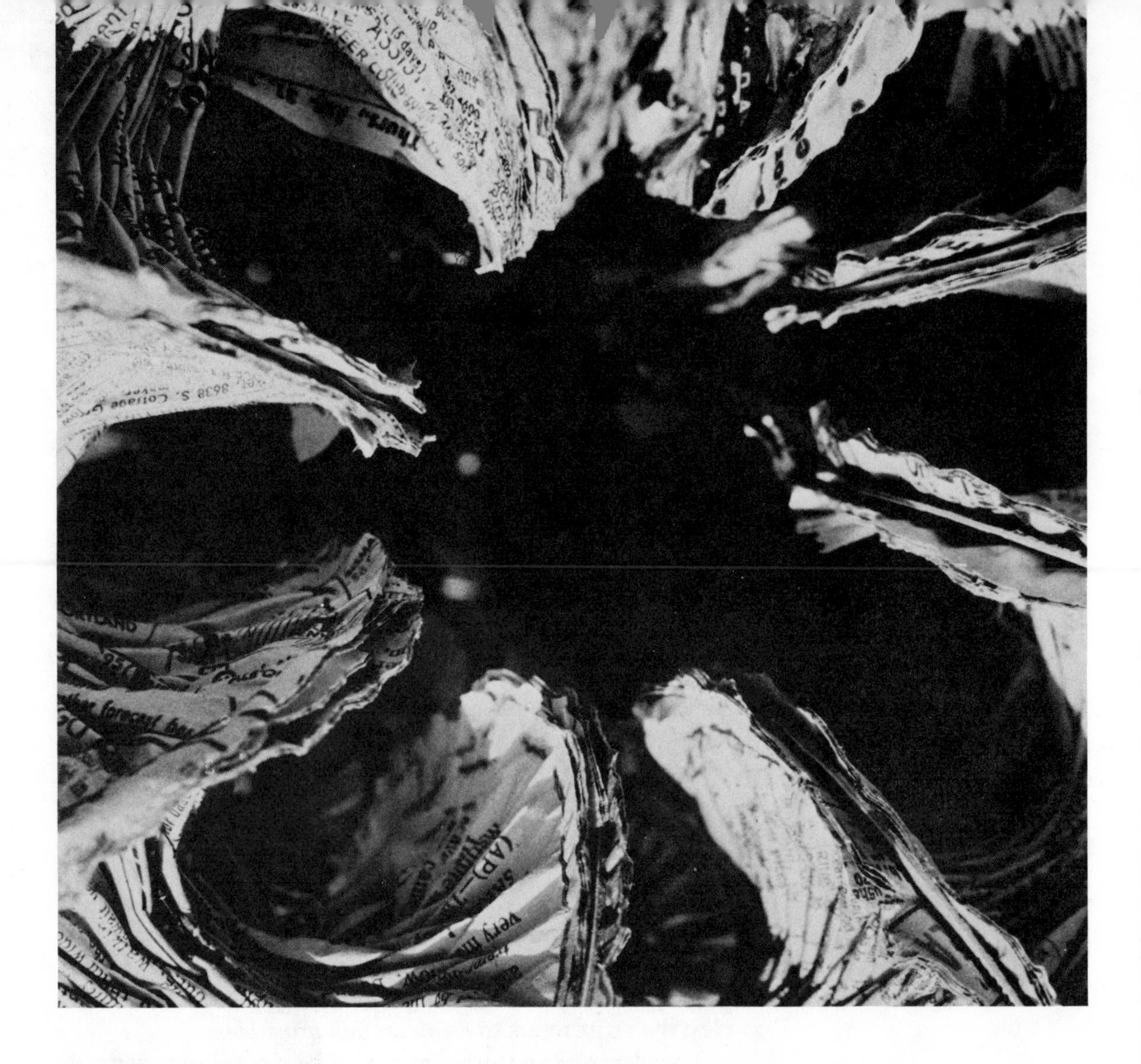

Newspaper Sculpture. (Detail) James Higa. A paper-crimping method results in repeat patterns and textures in a radiating design that suggests a mystery in its dark interior. Photo, Mel Meilach

The *principles* are considered *unity, rhythm, variety, repetition, balance, contrast, harmony,* and *direction.*

Learning how these concepts relate and interrelate is, to the artist, as exciting and challenging as solving mathematical problems is to the mathematician. The results can be creative, flexible, and inventive because of the infinite possibilities available.

The key to creating design lies in the unique *choices* one can make from the infinite potential everywhere. *Choice* is the key. The ultimate goal is learning to make a **creative choice** as opposed to an **ordinary choice.** This is a choice that can be learned; it is not an innate act, an act of some preguided mystical inheritance. The act of making creative choices is based on accepting or rejecting various criteria, evaluation, and re-evaluation through creative and learned judgment. The process of choice necessarily involves deci-

sion making. Each person's choice and judgment is affected by his individual viewpoint, his experiences, and his imaginative rearrangement of the elements he sees. Design is based, not necessarily on the newness of a form, but rather on the restructuring of the familiar to create something different.

A Palm Tree. Nature's patterning illustrates half-drop repeats in the limbs. The palm fronds and their repeated shadows are a source of design inspiration. Photo, Mel Meilach

How does this evolve? Let's imagine a tree. Each person's past experiences relate to his response to the concept of "tree." Let's assume a person had only seen an apple tree. To him, that would be his visualization of all trees. But as he expands his knowledge of trees, he learns that they vary tremendously; some trees are long and narrow, some short and squat; the leaves differ and the arrangement of the branches vary. If he were to design a tree, it would be based on combining and organizing, then selecting parts from the tree forms he is familiar with into his own interpretation, or expression, of a tree.

Spherical Three Part Construction. (Detail) Judith I. Kleinberg. Brass and copper were worked in knotless netting. Illustrates repeat pattern in varying sizes and materials. Photo, Royal A. Lyons

The lesson to be learned is that the more knowledge you gather and the more you observe, the greater is your vocabulary of visual images and the better able you are to make unique creative choices. This is true of all forms of expression whether literary, musical, or visual. All require that the creator organize his mental images and knowledge into some kind of order.

The artist has such a compendium of stimuli from which to draw, it is not surprising that creating a new order from what he sees presents a problem. He must learn to recognize the things that will expand his knowledge, to "see" them in terms of the *elements* and *principles* they exhibit, and then to digest and interpret them as creative design. It requires each person's viewpoint to rearrange his surroundings imaginatively and differently from that of another person.

Where does one look for design? Almost everywhere.

II. Sea Shell Hanging. (Detail) Janet McNinch. Knotless netting and crochet utilize many contrasts: textures, sizes, negative spaces, tight and loose areas. Photo, Edwin K. McNinch

Both nature and man have organized their creations into an order that can be called design. You will find design in a palm tree, in fruits and vegetables, in a wire structure, a netted hanging, a lumberyard, a building, and in two- and three-dimensional wood carvings. All contain an orderly arrangement of dot, line, shape, rhythm, although the materials, the size, and the purpose may differ vastly.

Compare the patterning of the ringed circular grooves of the tree trunk with the cratered folds in the newspaper sculpture. Or the open "airy" sky behind the tree in contrast to the enclosed dark space within the core of the paper sculpture.

The similarity between the organization of space in a wire-looped structure and of the fiber netting suggest a grapevine or webbed structure from nature. Each exhibits a variation of scale and a repetition of motif that are inherent in the order of the universe.

Stacked Lumber. A photographer's selected viewpoint of lumber stacked in a lumberyard shows alternating bands of middle and dark values and repeat rectangular patterns in different number and size sequences. Regular repeat pattern. Photo, Student, School of The Art Institute of Chicago

Photography depends on the ability of the artist to recognize design in everyday objects, then carefully select or rearrange what he sees to form a composition. He critically chooses his subject and then eliminates, through the viewer of his camera, any portions he may consider uninteresting. By knowing and controlling the technical means—the mechanism of his camera, in the case of the photographer—he decides on his design. He can alter the focus of the lens, plan a double exposure, blur foregrounds or backgrounds, or manipulate the texture of the print itself. During the entire creative process he constantly chooses and judges what he wants for the final result. This choice is based on the subconscious and conscious attention to the elements of his art.

Design is often influenced by the materials and techniques the artist selects. A wood carver's tools are his mechanical limits. The widths and shapes of his gouges

Stacked Lumber in Lumberyard. (Double exposure) The spacing of values and line patterning create a composition that could also inspire designs in other media—painting, printmaking, fabrics, and so forth.

dictate the pattern or design of his carving. If he selects wood for his design, and adheres to the mechanical confines imposed, he should design for the inherent quality of the wood. He should not try to make the wood look like ceramics or metal, for example. Nor should the ceramist or metalworker strive to make his work appear as wood. In selecting design, then, one must also consider the medium being used and the limits imposed by it. It is advisable to develop the strengths of a particular medium when developing a design for it.

The organization of space is another factor the designer must deal with. It can be the blank space on a sheet of paper that must be developed as a two-dimensional design. It can be environmental space which must be considered when creating a three-dimensional object such as a sculpture, a pot, or a building. There are two types of space which will be referred to throughout the book:

The Blacksmith. (Woodcut) Ernst Ludwig Kirchner. German. 1880. When carefully analyzed, this composition is found to contain the elements of dot, line, texture, shape, and value, all repeated, balanced, and unified in a harmonious total. Courtesy, The Art Institute of Chicago Collection, Gift of Print and Drawing Club

Carved Coconut Cup. Huon Gulf, New Guinea. The native wood carver subconsciously incorporates the same elements and principles as does a sophisticated artist like Kirchner. Courtesy, Field Museum of Natural History

Positive space is that space which is occupied.

Negative space is the air space which surrounds an object. For example, a doughnut occupies positive space; the hole in the doughnut represents negative space.

In addition to the design elements, there are also variables that affect the design such as the size of the elements and how they contrast, and the position, direction, number, intervals, and density of each. When you create a design, the degree of change in any one element causes a corresponding change in its relationship to the others and to the total design. For instance, alter the size, position, and color of a shape in relation to another shape and it will affect each shape plus other portions of the design.

All the facets mentioned will be clarified in the following chapters. You will discover how to create order from many visual images; and this order equals design. The basis for design is in every component part of nature and in the totality of the universe: All things relate. Therefore, the logical starting point for planning organization is to discover how you can create designs from nature.

CHAPTER 2

Designs from Nature

Our natural environment is an abundant and exciting source for design. Nature, concerned first with the unit of structure, also provides infinite relationships that are inherently the elements and principles of design.

The cycles of nature emphasize a natural balance that becomes a *harmony*. *Unity* occurs in the interplay between foreground and background in an organic form. Each part enhances and becomes an integral portion of the whole. The cycles of nature themselves provide a *rhythm*. *Variety* is achieved by *contrasts* of rhythm that lead to the principle of *balance*. *Contrasts* also occur between large and small, bright and dull, and they *balance* each other. You will discover *variety* in organic lines, in their heights and widths, their tones of light and dark, size and shape, colors and textures. When you analyze nature's forms for design, you should focus on the interrelationships of dot, line, shape-form-space, color-light, value, and texture.

Designs in nature exist in seedheads, leaves, branches, honeycombs, in bony fish and animal skeletons, and everywhere you think to look. The microscope, camera lens, and telescope help expand our field of observation to include delicate colors, structures, and textures of the minutest forms.

Using these instruments and your bare eye, observe fluid and angular outlines and inner structural lines of animal, vegetable, and mineral forms. Observe the texture and the circular patterns in a piece of coral and in the repeated geometric patterns of reptile skins. You will also find that simple, pure shapes are echoed, with variations, in all the substructures.

Sailfish. Dot, line, texture, and contour are evident and a source for design. Photo, Mel Meilach

Palm Tree. Your relation to an object can suggest different ideas. Learning to observe nature's patterning, at different ranges, will result in a broad range of design choices. (Far left) Palm fronds from a distance. (Above) At closer range, the stems form fanlike patterning. (Above right) Still closer, another appearance evolves—the stems appear closer and tighter.
(Right bottom) Very close viewpoint shows the stem's growth pattern as an interwoven design. All viewpoints and aspects of the photo could be used to inspire line, rhythm, repeat, texture, and other necessary design components.

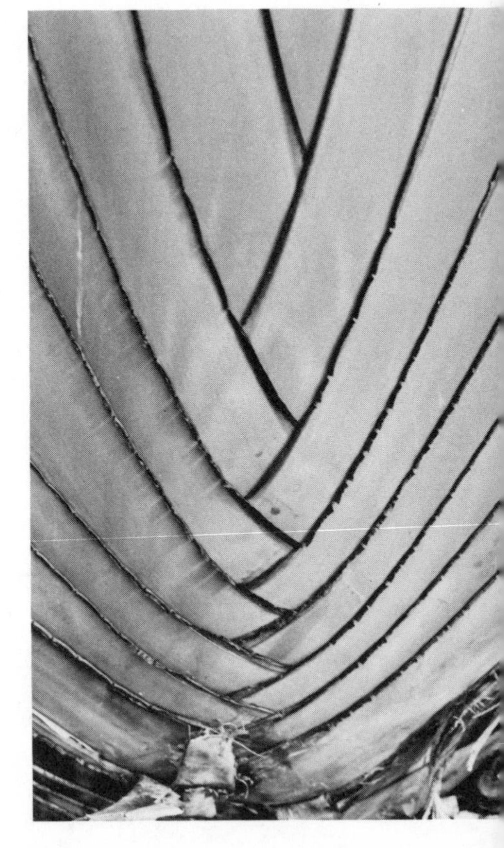

The designer must also look to nature for subtleties that occur. The brown of a tree trunk is a good example. There are tremendous color variations in the brown . . . from mauve-brown to rich gray-green-brown to brown-black, all in one tree trunk. The subtle transitions from hue to hue result in color harmony.

The trunk and leaves of a palm tree, tree bark, duck feathers, bones, and shells all provide their unique contribution as design resource materials. You, the designer, must interject the human elements of selection, rejection, emphasis, interpretation, and composition upon these borrowings from nature.

Jellyfish. Variation and repetition within a circle and of circles to one another.

Tree Trunk Burl. Swirling oval and circular repeat lines with dot, texture, and rhythm are all in nature and can be creatively selected by the craftsman for his purposes. Photo, Lois Constantine

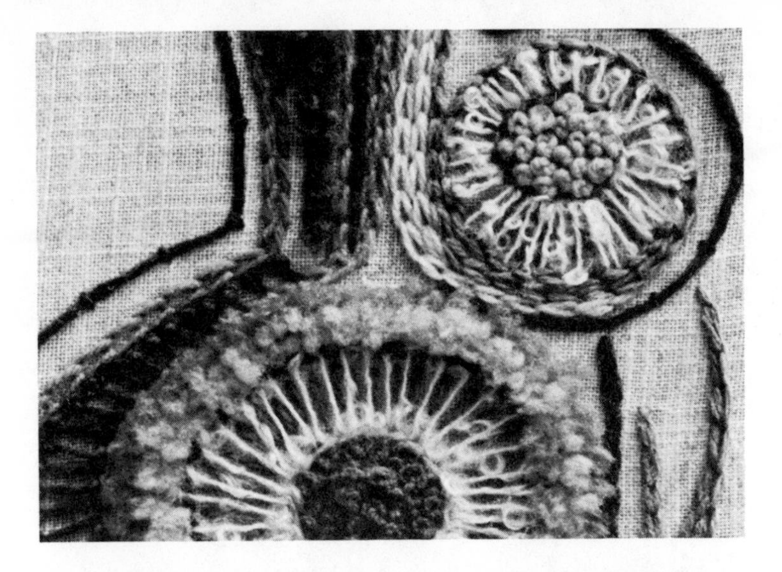

Stitchery. (Detail) Siol. Patterns are similar to those in the Jellyfish (opposite).

Ozymandias. Gillian Bradshaw-Smith. Soft sculpture of stuffed fabric with ink drawing has a feeling similar to the patterning in the photo (opposite) or the hide of an elephant. Courtesy, artist

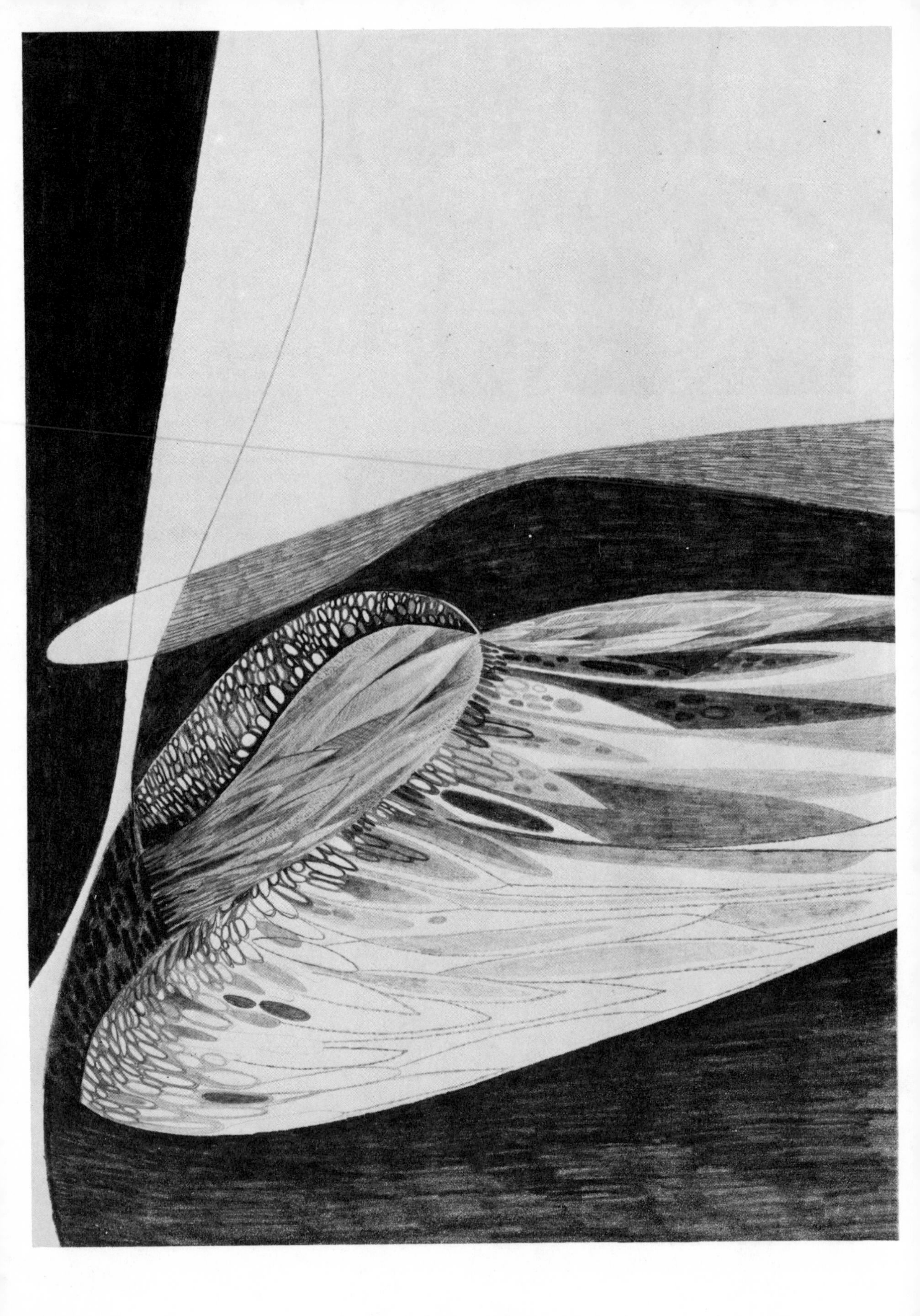

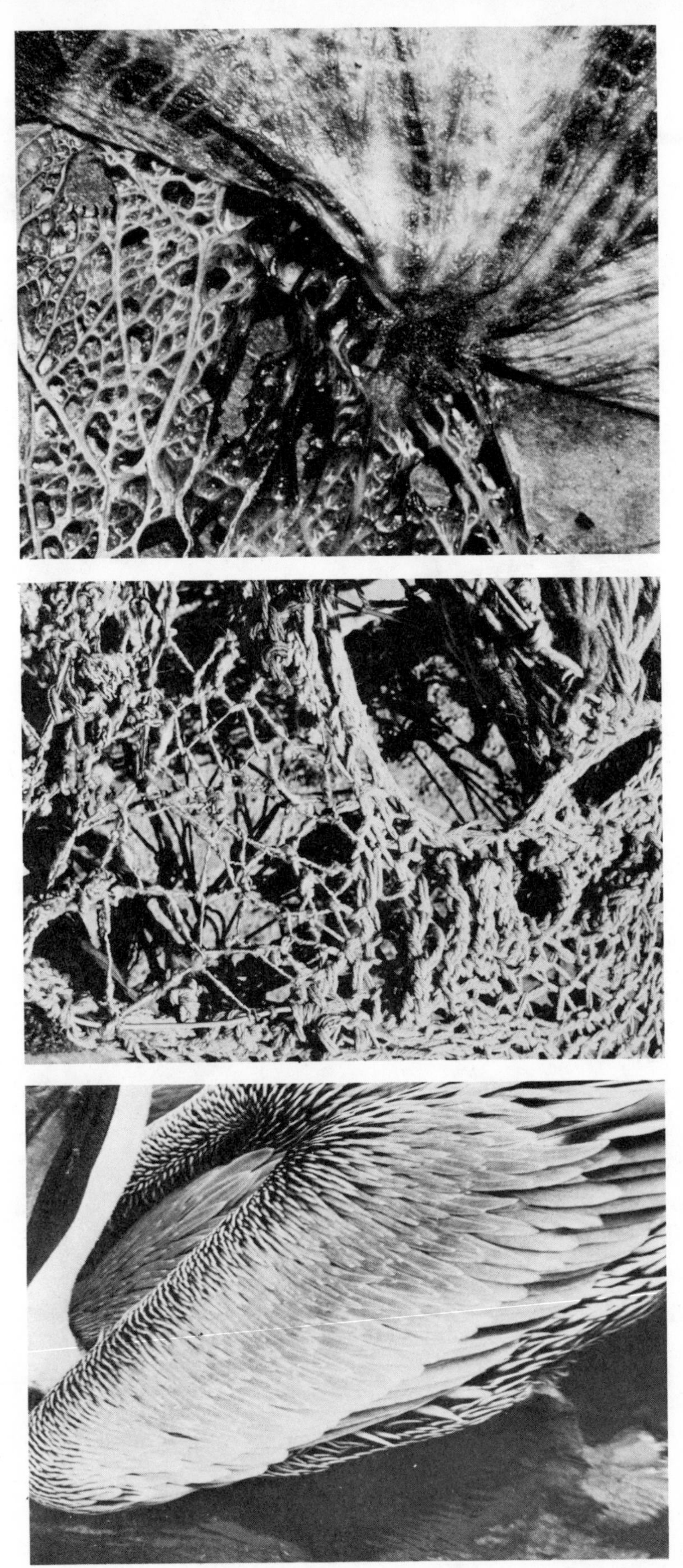

Seaweed patterns have been a favorite design source for artists for centuries . . .

. . . such as the patterning in the layers of woven threads in the detail of a non-loom-woven construction by Joyce Wexler.

Duck. One must study nature's patterns close up to recognize the rich use of design elements. Observe how portions have been interpreted in dots, lines, values, at left.

Variation on a Duck. (Opposite) Bill Hinz. 10¼″ high, 7″ wide. Pencil drawing. An abstract composition inspired by the duck photograph (right bottom).

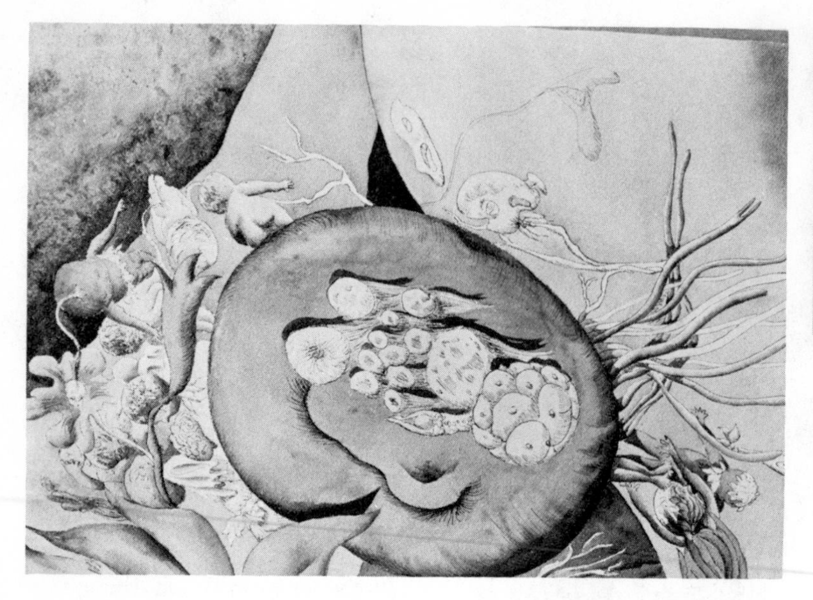

Drawings based on bones and shell forms by Serene Flax. Top is detail of full drawing at bottom. Shell and bone forms are an excellent stimulus for designs.

Eileen Bernard uses the shells themselves in a necklace design. Sand dollar and cowrie shells are combined with linen thread worked in macramé square knots.

Rocks and Tree Trunk. Photo, Jay Hinz

Rocks and Tree Trunk. Jay Hinz. 5½″ high, 8″ wide. Ink drawing. Design based upon inspiration from the photograph above, using mainly dots and lines to achieve different values.

EXERCISES

NATURAL SHAPES—amoeboid or free form.

You may have to research these forms in any biology or botany book.

1 Use black, white, or gray construction paper. Cut *flat shapes* to resemble the following in their *simplest* contour:

A. Six different leaves (oak, maple, elm)

B. A crystalline structure

C. Three microscopic or molecular patterns (blood platelets or cellular structures)

D. Two varied snowflakes.

2 Make *detail* drawings from any or all of the following: Bird-feather patterns, coral, fish scales, insect wings, reptiles, rock veining, sea shells, sea urchin, seed pods, snakes, starfish, tree bark, weeds.

3 Make skeletal and growth pattern sketches of any of the below, using the entire skeletal structure or part: Animals, fish, ferns, flowers, leaves.

4 Take at least two of the two-dimensional (2D) shapes you have cut out of construction paper. Place tracing paper on top, and, using your research, develop a line and texture pattern that compliments the form and subject.

5 Use black, white, and gray values and develop pencil designs from the photographs illustrated: Tomatoes, artichoke, figs, coral. Designs can be based on the entire photograph, or on a selected portion. They should incorporate several of the elements (dot, line, shape, texture, value, and color) and follow an:

A. *Organization* (The relationship of the part to the whole): Size, Number, Proportion, Interval, Density, Sequence, Proximity, Position, Rhythm (movement, direction), Continuity (closure or openness).

B. *Balance:* Tension

C. *Harmony*

D. *Unity*

E. *Contrast:* This refers to the extremes including similarities and differences, uniformity and variation, sameness and uniqueness.

Tomatoes.

Artichoke.

Figs.

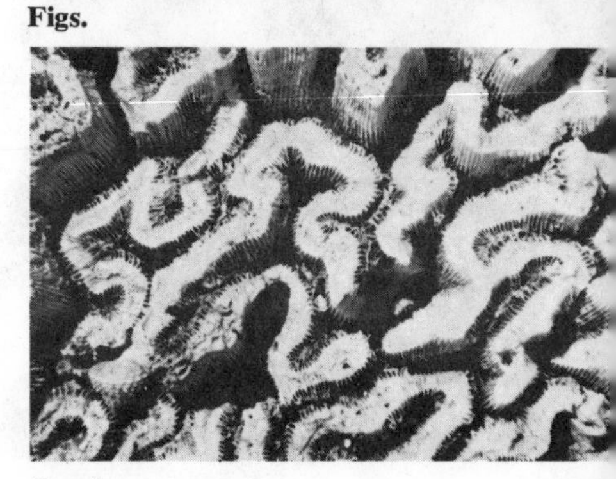

Coral.

CHAPTER 3

Man-made Design and Point of View

Design, as applied or created by man, is connected with his mental processes. It involves education, awareness, sensitivity, and selectivity, all mind-centered acts. When you begin to concentrate on man-made objects as inspiration for new design potential, *the* most significant factor is your point of view, or how you observe. Point of view is the result of perspective and perception, sensitivity and selectivity.

You can actively and purposely learn to expand your point of view. First, it is necessary to become aware of various ways you might look at things. Education and training can provide an entire new way of seeing. You will rediscover the excitement of investigation, alteration, and change, whenever you choose to apply these newly found skills.

You must learn to critically analyze to find new relationships. Take an area out of its intended context and isolate it or juxtapose it with another area taken from something else for one point of view. Eliminate total portions of an area, or emphasize certain parts to the exclusion of others, or add something that correlates to the rest to offer deviation from the original. Distort an object or objects to provide another point of view. Alter the scale of one or more elements within one frame of reference to obtain another point of view. Then try to change one perspective to "non-reality" to inspire another means of interpretation.

Brick Architectural Surface. A man-made design is also a source for designs in several media. Photo, Mel Meilach

Storage Tanks. An unusual viewpoint helps discover unusual design potential. An upward movement creates a perspective diminution. Straight linear perspective and curved area provide detail interest that offsets the bulky curved shapes. Photo, Mel Meilach

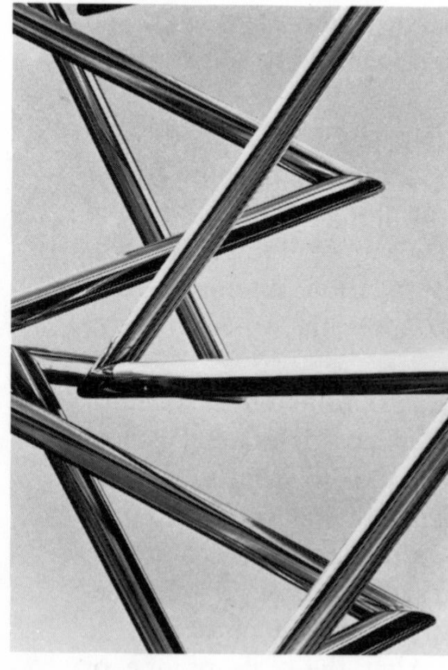

A detail only of an aluminum sculpture might suggest thrusting angles and relationships of negative space.

The sequence of perceptual analysis begins with the *general* field of focus. This narrows toward a *particular* detail of interest. During this process of creative decision-making (acceptance, emphasis, and rejection), you must exercise intense concentration to enable you to see the familiar aesthetically. This process goes beyond mere identification and classification. It enables you to recognize the subtle variations of color, size, shape, and individual differences within a given range of view. Imaginative manipulation of this chosen "field" will create an original image, a combination of visual experiences, and unique interpretation.

The camera is a tool for extending visual scope and scrutinizing your immediate environment. Close attention should be given to the commonplace . . . the rhythmical patterning in brick, the dynamic vertical perspective formed by the windows in a tall building, a chair, a feather, brain coral, fish scales, fruits, and vegetables.

High-Rise. A design could be made entirely from an object viewed in an unexpected way. Or it could be only the beginning for a design. Photo, Jay Hinz

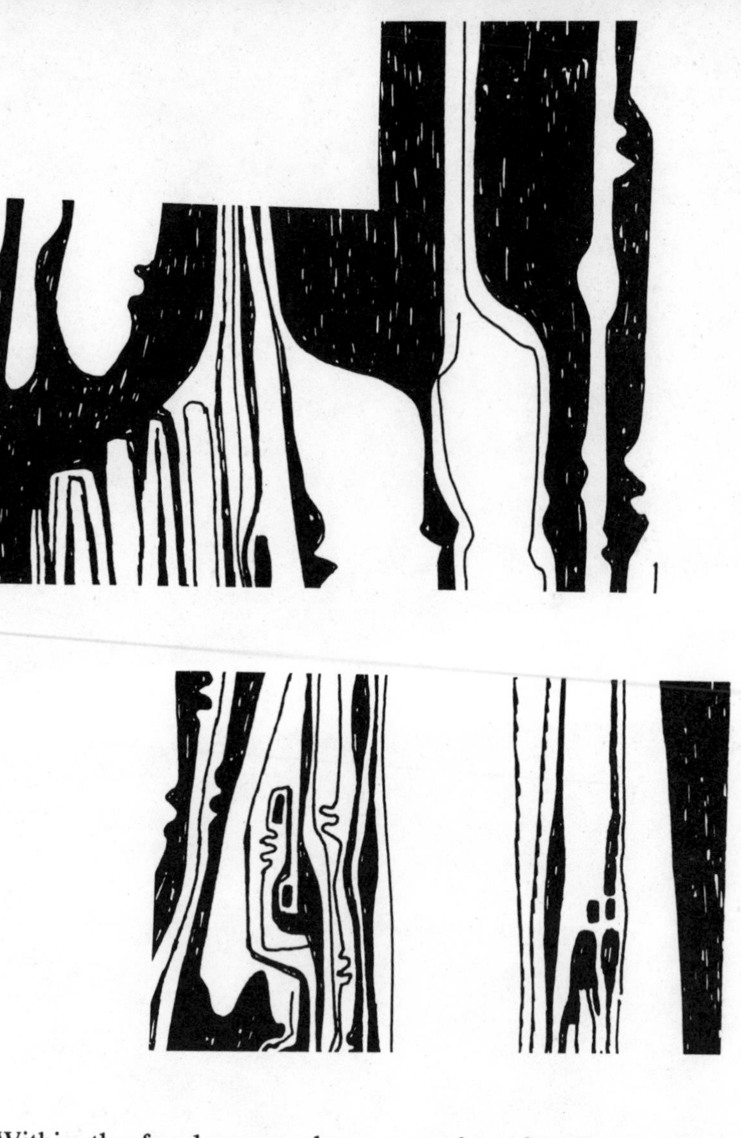

Assemblage. Bill Hinz. An entire ink drawing was photostated. Then parts were cut out to suggest and develop new designs.

Within the focal range, the area and angle of concentration are selectively screened by the photographer and the camera lens. Distortions can be capitalized upon with the aid of special micro, fish-eye, and telephoto lenses. Scientific photographic equipment can zero in on the designs in micropatterns of a cell fragment to macropatterns of the universe.

The point of view via the camera is similar to the process of abstracting, which also can be effectively applied to man-made sources to arrive at good design. The point of view must first be determined. It should then be drawn exactly as seen. Next, each component should be sketched separately. This should be followed by a drawn skeletal structure and textural sketches. Finally, these drawings should be simplified and rearranged into your own combination, placing emphasis and contrast upon some parts, eliminating others, cross-sectioning any part, or repeating any segment. Ultimately, as with the camera, your own de-

Chairforms. Jay Hinz. Photograph. Ordinary forms can provide design inspiration by highlighting some parts and eliminating others.

sign will result. Always remember to employ the elements and principles whenever you are organizing any design.

Developing your visual awareness will provide you with the tools necessary for clarifying, understanding, and sharpening your sensibilities. Continual sharpening of the senses leads to a greater knowledge for understanding and discovering the infinite sources for design.

The same source of inspiration can stimulate as many different designed responses as there are designers using it. This idea is investigated further in Chapter 13, "Sources and Interpretation." The creative designer rediscovers natural and man-made genre objects continuously. He absorbs these objects through all of his senses. He discovers the hairline cracks and pores in a piece of wood, the minute specks in its textural surface. Each reassociation, with renewed attention to the same source, will sharpen his perception of that object and enlarge his visual vocabulary for creative interpretation.

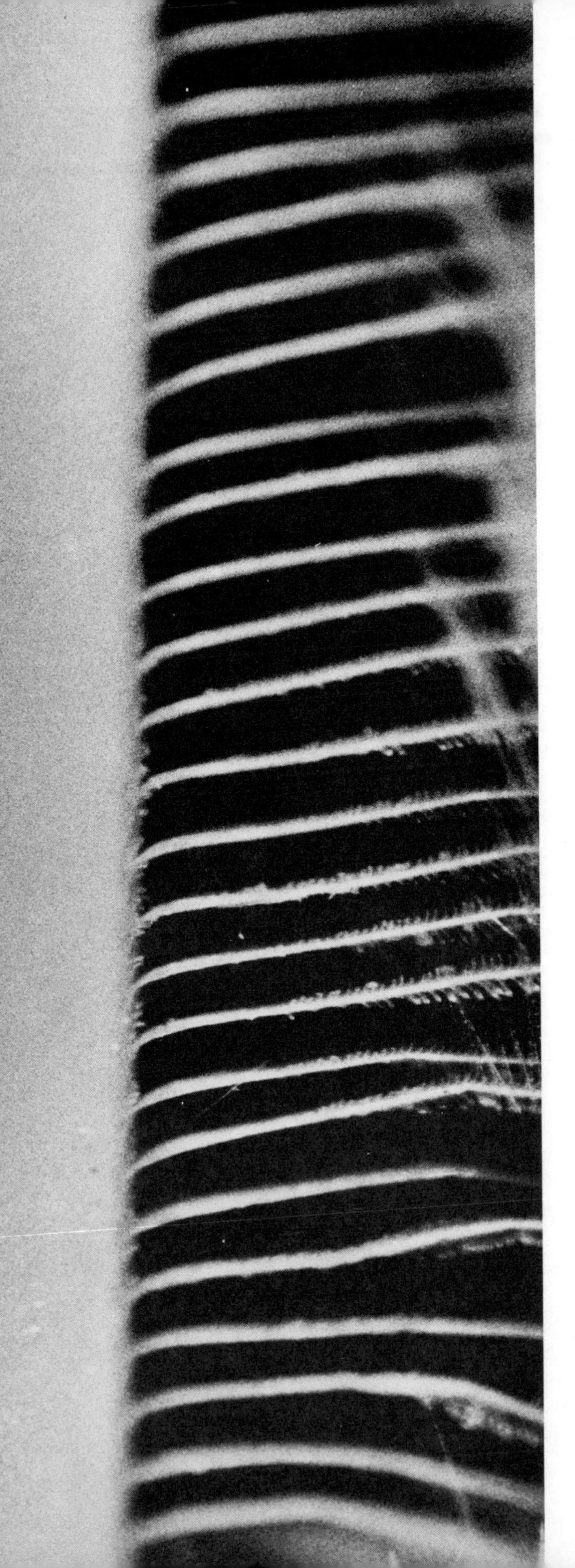

Sewer Covers. (Opposite) Viewing everyday objects out-of-context can provide unsuspected, new relationships of design elements. Photo, Mel Meilach

Feather Detail. Magnification of minute details can reveal startling design potential. Photo, Student, School of The Art Institute of Chicago

Leather Scraps. Murry Kusmin. The repeat patterns from cut-out leather scraps on top of one another can suggest a variety of ideas depending on the different ways you look at them. See interpretation on opposite page.

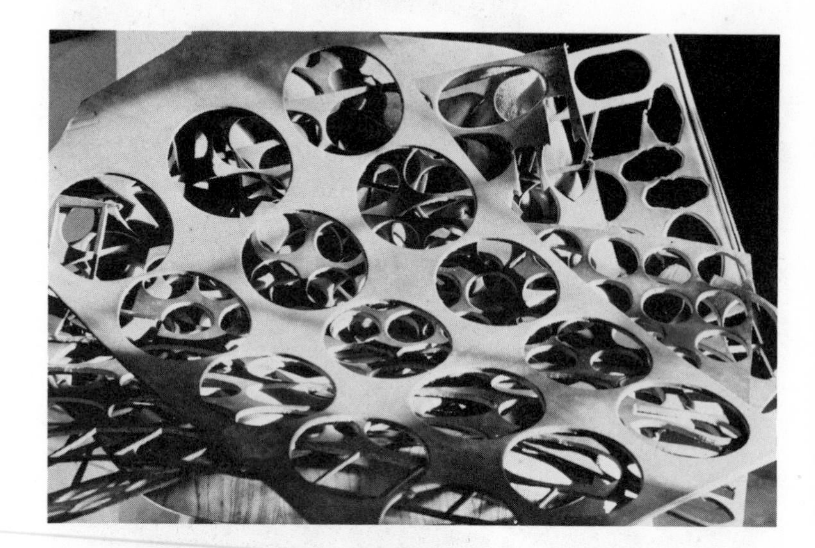

Detail within one hole.

Several overlaid sheets illustrate line, negative, and positive shapes.

The same area turned sideways suggests other patterns.

EXERCISES

Problems:

1 As the basis for a design, select a photograph you have taken, or one from a magazine, of a man-made item or structure. Isolate an unusual area and eliminate the rest. Interpret this into a design. Whether photographing or looking, try a different viewing angle—straight up, straight down, upside down, or a severe or unusual angle.

2 Enlarge the above design to 8″×12″.

A. The shapes should become large and simple, and the lines, by virtue of their enlarged thickness, should become narrow *shapes*.

B. Match the colors and values and paint the flat tones in tempera on illustration board.

3 Take the same photograph and duplicate it four times by photocopy. Cut each duplicate apart in different ways. Reassemble all of them into four new design interpretations. Glue the pieces onto a backing sheet.

4 Cut a 2″×3″ rectangular hole in a 6″×8″ piece of paper. Look through the hole and maneuver it about the room, or the environment, until you decide upon an interesting composition. Take any ordinary object out of context, making the portions thereof unrecognizable. Sketch the lines, shapes, values, colors, and textures you see within this format. Use this as a beginning for the development of a design.

5 Seek out six everyday man-made items and organize them into one unified design using the elements and principles.

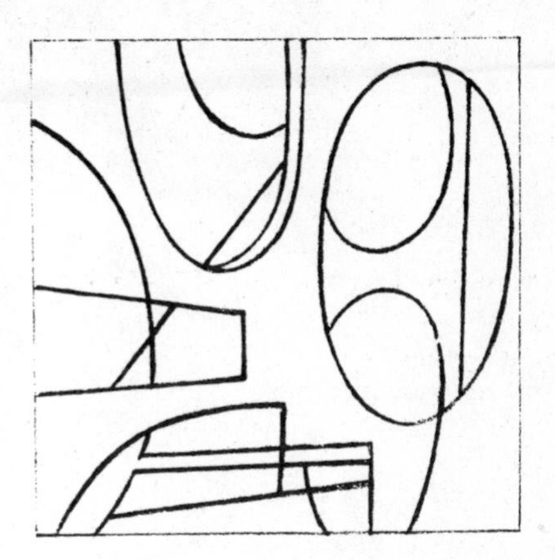

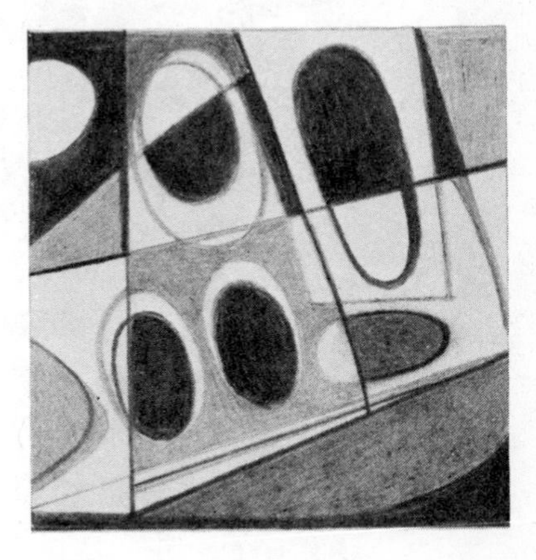

Leather Scraps. Jay Hinz. The above designs were inspired by the leather scraps at left. (Top) A linear pencil design. (Center) A pencil design showing shapes, planes, and value relationships. (Below) Another pencil drawing from the photos at left.

CHAPTER 4

Dot

How an image is formed is limited only by the types of surfaces, media, and tools available to the artist. A small, single dot is the simplest unit of image formation. It provides the symbolism of the texture of the universe—the sand, the stars. The dot, to the artist, is like the atom to the scientist. Therefore, it is the first element of design.

The dot exists everywhere. In nature, the most minute dot in the micro-organism of a cellular structure is visible only through microscopic investigation. In animals, it is found in the camouflage of insects and beasts. In plants, the dot may be recognized as the spotting of the tiger lily or as the termite holes in a tree trunk. In minerals, dot markings are visible on rocks and stones. A dot may be a focal point at the intersection of two lines, a pupil in an eye, a skin pore, or a pin point.

The potential of the simple, single dot is fantastic. It can expand and contract to activate its surrounding areas. It indicates location. A group of dots can be articulate or staccato. It begins to suggest direction and rhythm. Dots can overlap, thicken toward a specific area, be scattered at random, be of even or uneven pressure, or of equal or unequal size. By manipulating and controlling dots, you can achieve a concentration of value areas to communicate a sense of form and space. Grouped together, dots may visually combine into a compact shape. The control of shape and value with dots is a tool for the creation of any complex form.

Control of the element of dot is a key to the investigation of light and dark. Isolated white areas surrounded by other values will provide the contrast of light and dark that is instrumental in the creation of spatial illusion.

The dot as a technique for creative expression was evolved by Georges Seurat and called "pointillism." His best-known example is "La Grande Jatte," 1884–86, which is composed of carefully applied equal-sized dots of the primary colors.

Growth. Bill Hinz. Ink drawing. Value densities are interpreted with dots only.

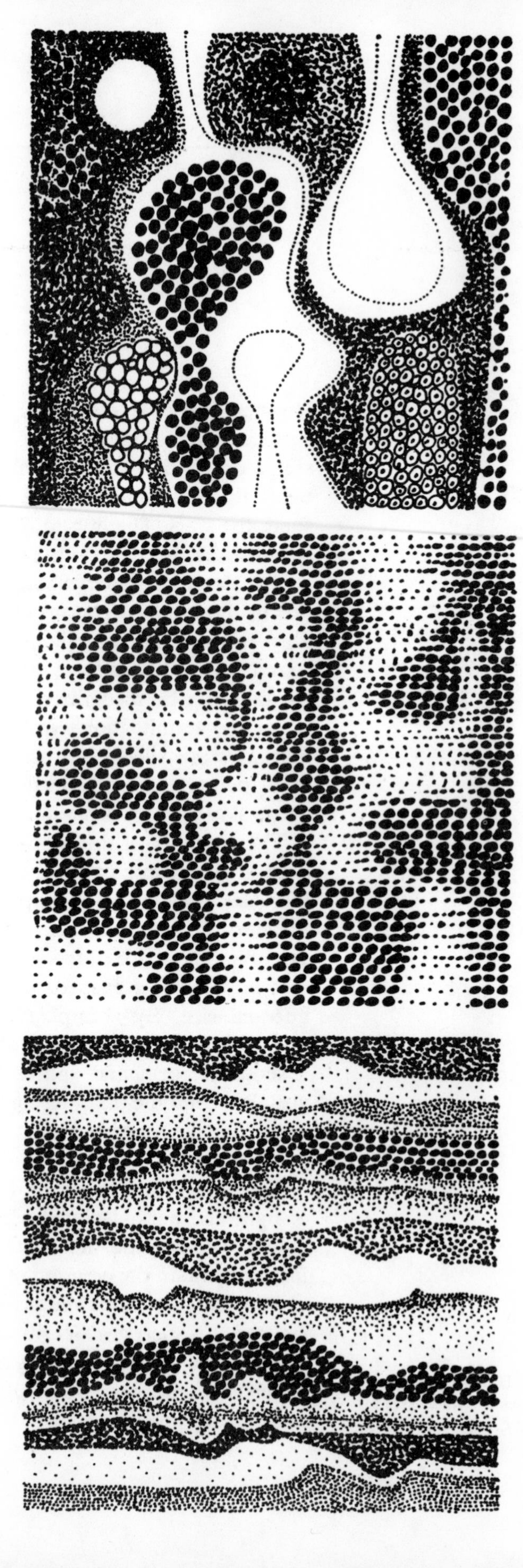

Dot Design I. Bill Hinz. Ink drawing. The design *elements,* shape, value, and texture, interrelate through the *principles* of design. An asymmetric balance illustrates harmony, thus unity, through the use of repetition, variation, rhythm, and dominance, in size, position, and density of the dots.

Dot Design II. Bill Hinz. Ink drawing. Movement.

Dot Design III. Bill Hinz. Ink drawing. Bands of various curved contours with alternation of values.

Dot Design I. Jay Hinz. Ink drawing. Positive two-dimensional shapes with negative spaces. One illusionary three-dimensional orb.

Dot Design II. Jay Hinz. Ink drawing. Black, white, and gray with straight- and curved-edged positive shapes and negative spaces.

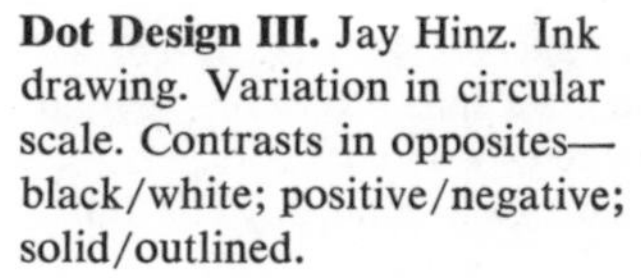

Dot Design III. Jay Hinz. Ink drawing. Variation in circular scale. Contrasts in opposites—black/white; positive/negative; solid/outlined.

Jewelry. Bob Christiaansen. Cast-gold pin with cultured pearls. The negative dots drilled through the metal are repeated in the positive dots of the pearls.

Flower. A real flower could be interpreted as being composed of small three-dimensional circles which could be drawn as dots in a two-dimensional design. Photo, Mel Meilach

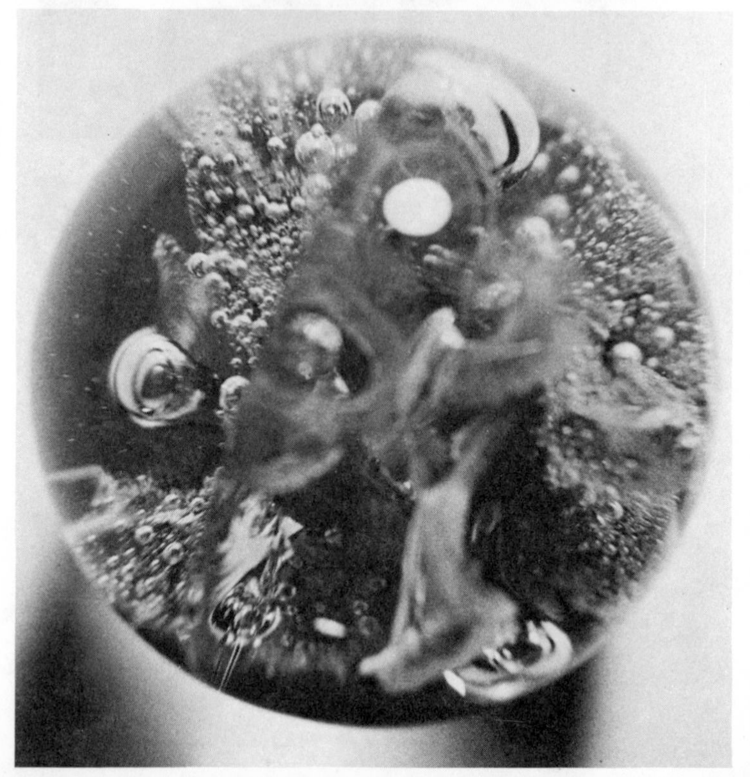

Glass Paperweight. Kent Ipsen. A blown-glass sphere contains myriad dot bubbles within its core. Photo, Jay Hinz. Collection, Jay and Bill Hinz

EXERCISES

Encrusted Tree Trunk. (Detail) Harve Schaefer. 24″ high. The pattern applied to this organic form consists entirely of nails of various sizes and metals. The nailheads produce a dot texture. Courtesy, artist

In the following exercises, note particularly what happens as dots get closer and closer to one another and begin to group. Do you see lines? Shapes? Forms? The desirable goal is to develop control over the grouping patterns, over the lights, grays, and darks, over the sizes and shapes of the dots. Do not attempt too large an area. Patience, perseverance, and precision are essential. As in every learned skill, the more time you devote to practice, the more controlled and predictable will be your results.

Materials: A black felt-tipped pen. White typing paper.

Method:

1 Rule off a number of 4″ squares.

2 Holding the pen vertically, apply even pressure as you carefully press down, leave a mark, and lift up.

3 Holding the pen vertically, tap the tip of the pen against the paper rapidly and repeatedly. A more random dotting will occur and the size of the dots may alter somewhat from the precision of the previous method.

Exercise:

1 Using Method 3, try any random scattering of dots.

2 Using Method 2, try to control the density of the dots. Begin by connecting the dots on the left side of the square and producing a total black area. *Gradually* spread dots apart, creating the illusion of gray. Continue spacing the dots farther and farther apart until you finally arrive at the right side of your square which should remain pure white. The transition from black to gray to white should be as subtle as possible. Go slowly and strive for control.

3 Using both Methods 2 and 3, create a pattern of dots to include a build-up of strong dark and isolated white areas.

4 Select and analyze several postcard reproductions of well-known works of art and isolate any dot design to recognize how it is employed.

5 Punch out dots from black, white, and gray construction paper with a paper punch. Organize them into a two-dimensional design, altering the shape of the dots whenever necessary for contrast.

6 Plan a three-dimensional design composed of dots. The structural material selected, such as the knots of macramé, nailheads, or stones, will determine the type and size of dot.

Ring. Park Chambers. Gold and silver. The various-sized metal spheres create an all-over-dot, textural-relief surface and pattern. Collection, Bill Hinz

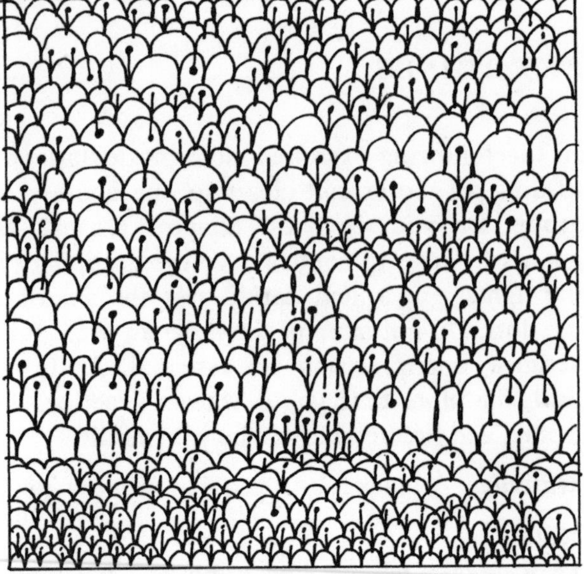
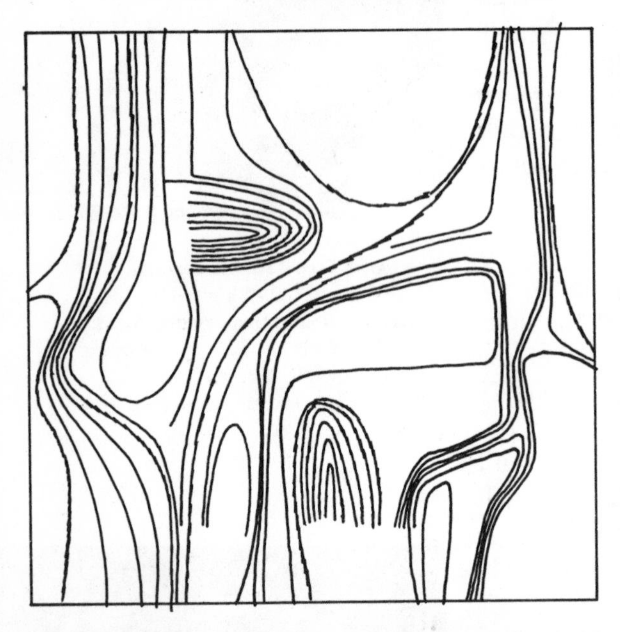
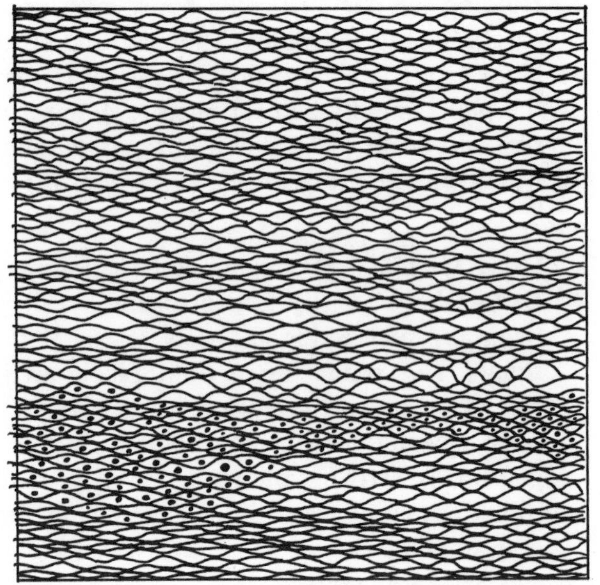

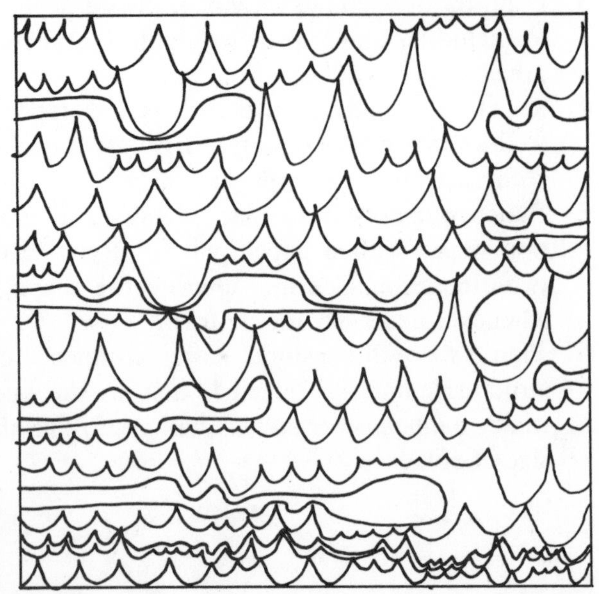

CHAPTER 5

Line

Line is the means by which communication is recorded. The most obvious example of it is seen in lettering and calligraphy. These forms of communication are an outgrowth of the cave drawings of prehistoric man. Even today line is used to create symbols.

A line results from the connection of a series of points. The dimension of length is primary in that it implies an extension in a vertical, horizontal, diagonal, or curved direction. Each movement creates its own mood—static, tranquil, dynamic, voluptuous.

A *vertical* line identifies with gravitational pull.

A *horizontal* line suggests foundation. Together, they symsymbolize the balance of human experience and are called balanced oppositions of tensions.

Diagonal lines create a balanced suspension between unresolved tendencies toward the vertical and the horizontal.

Curved lines convey rhythm.

Lines have many functions. They can divide a flat space into any number of areas; they can create a two-dimensional design. Lines alone can provide the motif that is the basis for a design. They can create perspective and tonal value to give the illusion of three-dimensional space. Black and white lines close together are perceived as gray. The darkness or lightness of the gray is affected by the thickness of the lines and the amount of spacing between them. Lines may be repeated to build up shapes and forms and to simulate textures. A line may be calligraphic for surface enhancement or lines can define objects to suggest mass. When line encloses space and a shape results, it creates the illusion of volume.

Patterns. Bill Hinz. Ink drawings. Examples one and two utilize areas of line with open space, repetition, and variation. Examples three, four, five, and six are repeat patterns with variation in scale, density, and contour line. The element of dot has been added to examples one, four, and five. Notice the irregular placements.

Olvera Street. Jo Rebert. 22″ high, 30″ wide. Three-color linoleum print. The style of this print relies on the repeated contour line in different thicknesses and values. Courtesy, artist

Lines are important for expressing ideas, emotions, and moods. Lines may be either active or passive. An active repetition of sketchy lines in a gesture drawing suggests movement in space; the essence of the action is communicated while the details of observation and decoration are eliminated. A passive line is represented by the edge of contact between planes or surfaces. A line of continuity is formed when an edge of one shape continues beyond it to become the edge of an adjoining shape. A virtual line is one that is suggested by continuous repeated marks at regular intervals. This type of line relies upon optical connection to complete it.

A line may be a negative space between two buildings or a positive force describing the contour of a form. Contour drawing uses a single, continuous line to record the outline of the subject.

There are many types of lines. A rhythmic line may be drawn by varying the thickness within it. This may be accomplished by turning the nib of a lettering pen or by varying the pressure on a brush. Hatched lines may be made by building up rows of short strokes. Stripes and textured areas may be made by varying the thickness and grouping of the strokes. Blown lines may be made by drawing a heavy line with India ink and blowing sideways at it with

Fiber as Line. Barbara Manger. Line used in different lengths, angles, and spaces creates optical play and illusion. Photo, Richard Gross

a straw, forcing the ink to run randomly over the paper. A scratched line may be made with a needle or other sharp point. An incised line may be made by carving into a surface deeper than paper such as wood or linoleum.

A line may be a silken thread from a spider's web or a shimmering shaft of stainless steel.

The character of line partially depends upon the tool used to make it. Each kind of tool makes its own kind of line. Sticks, pencils, pens, brushes, burins, chalk, and silverpoint all produce lines uniquely their own. Most tools are available in differing shapes and sizes. Pencil lead comes in various hardnesses. Pencils are made from different substances such as graphite, charcoal, conte, and grease, each producing a different effect. Thick pigments produce a line quite different from one resulting from a fluid ink.

Surfaces can alter the character of the line produced upon it. Smooth papers permit a fluid line while toothed papers produce a blurry-edged one. Waxed paper, charcoal paper, rice paper, blotter paper, drawing paper, typewriter paper, tracing paper, vellum, tagboard, illustration board, and water-color paper should all be investigated to discover the unique possibilities inherent in each. Experiment with different media until you discover those which enable

The Little Equilibrist. Jacques Villon. 1914. Etching. Shapes are created by the different densities of vertical lines. Courtesy, The Art Institute of Chicago

you to communicate your ideas most emphatically and effectively.

The various tools should be used on each of the types of paper to include the broadest range of techniques. The same experiments should be done on both wet and dry paper. The extremes of possibilities should be investigated: thick lines, thin lines; delicate lines, bold lines; continuous lines, broken lines; sharp lines, blurred lines; angular lines, straight lines, curved lines; dark lines, light lines; lines made by a brush loaded with paint, dry-brush lines. When this sequence has been exhausted, begin by testing various combinations of lines beginning with alternating thick and thin lines or thick and thin areas occurring within the same line.

Continually practice and develop a controlled hand motion and pressure until you master the materials and techniques that produce creative lines.

Through line, the principles of design may be satisfied.

Icarus. Joseph Almyda. 1967. Approximately 40″ high, 50″ wide. Batik on silk. Dark lines are used to outline and accentuate shapes; the inner lines are lighter in value. Courtesy, American Craftsmen's Council

Faces. (Left above) Gloria Rigling. 48″ high, 36″ wide. Batik, tie-dye discharge, and redye. Yellow cotton. Dye colors: hot pink, red, and navy crackle. The delicate line preserves the original white fabric color by the use of hot wax applied with a tjanting tool. Courtesy, artist

Palette. Mary Bauermeister. 1966. 19¾" high, 12½" wide. Painting and raised assembled parts. Photo, Eric Pollitzer. Courtesy, Galeria Bonino, Ltd., New York

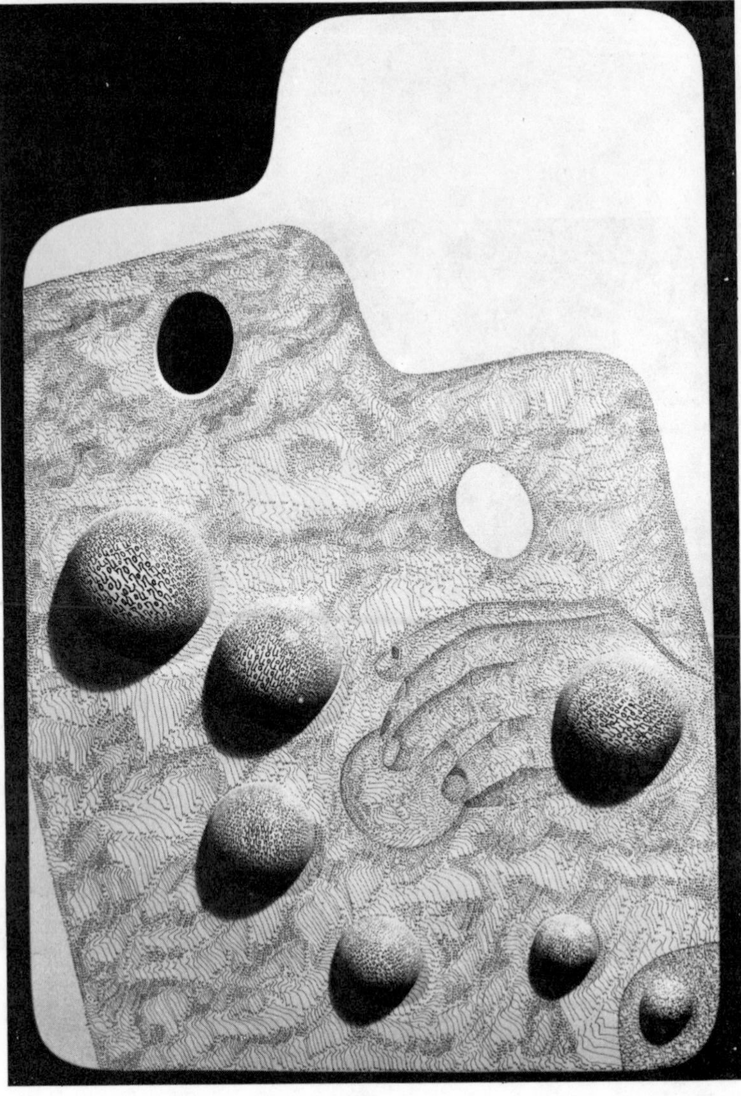

Calligraphic curved bands of line pattern cover the two-dimensional surface.

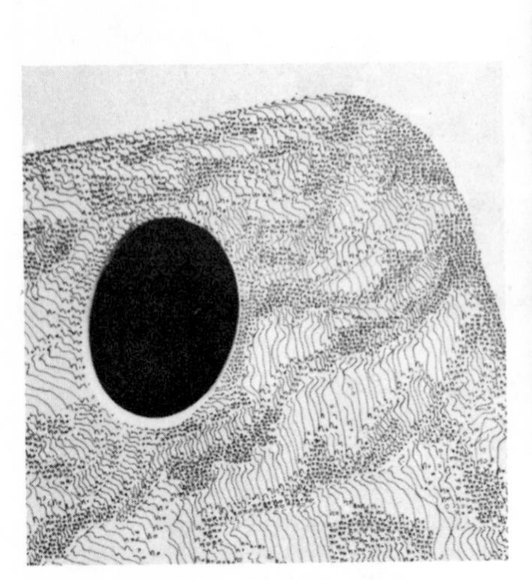

The calligraphic lines add the illusion of dimension to the hand and the round form defined on the two-dimensional surface. They add surface pattern to the relief half-round form.

Lines may be repeated to build up shapes, forms, and values. They may be outline. They may parallel one another for a harmonious effect or oppose one another for contrast. They may radiate from a point or converge upon it for emphasis. A diagonal line may offset the too monotonous balance of vertical and horizontal lines. A zigzag may create the desired effect. Line variation may include the long or short line, thick or thin line, jagged wavy or smooth straight line. It is seldom that only one kind of line is used in a design. More likely two or more types of line interweave throughout a design with varying degrees of harmony and contrast. Balance can be accomplished by the placement, grouping, and direction of lines. Lines can provide the unifying element that makes a composition a good design.

Palette, by Mary Bauermeister, shows a play in incongruities between the second and the third dimension and

Jewelry. Bob Christiaansen. Cast and forged sterling, with leather and carnelian stones.

The core of the piece is convex, completely covered with curvilinear incised design. The design expands on a circular theme.

The outer sterling-silver rim repeats the circular motif with raised lines and dots. The final outer backing is leather with a tooled incised line to carry through the lines in the silver.

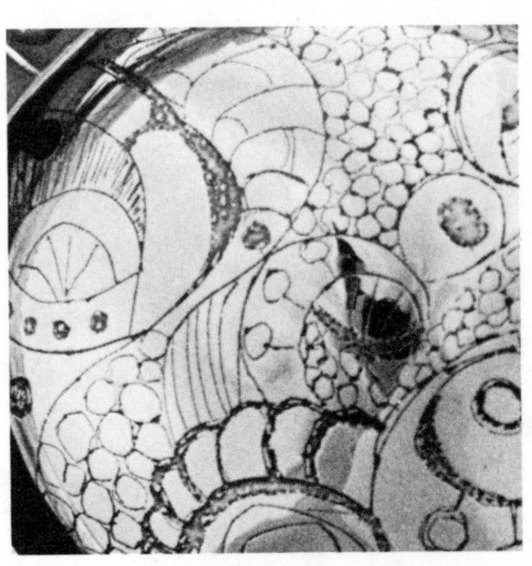

between negative and positive space. The concentration of calligraphic line segments creates a value and texture pattern. Rhythmical currents of lines are interrupted by the eruption of several three-dimensional half rounds. These flatten out into a two-dimensional circle developed through the same use of linear patterning. The controlled concentration of lines and value is responsible for the illusion of shape. The flat circle is elongated into elliptical voids. White is often considered to be "positive" or that which occupies space. However, both the white and the black ovals appear to be holes in the palette. Therefore, both appear to represent negative space. The variation of scale of the three-dimensional half rounds is emphasized by the corresponding change in scale in the visual pattern applied to these forms. This patterning provides an over-all unifying effect to the entire composition. The black and white starkness surrounding it emphasizes the subject.

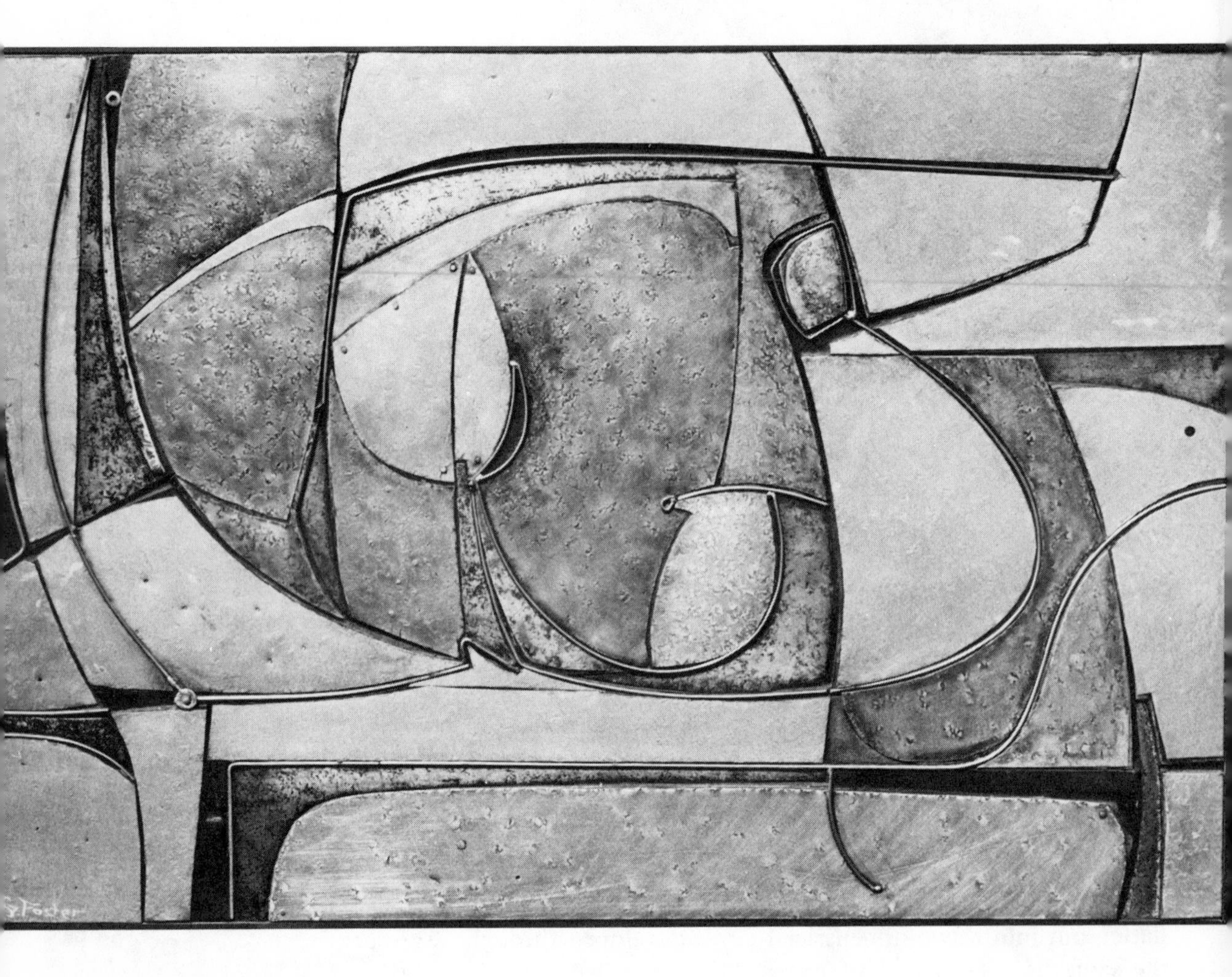

Metal Collage. George Foster. 1972. 18″ high, 23″ wide. The metal line pattern adds reinforcement to the shapes and unifies the composition. Photographed at the Collector's Showroom, Chicago

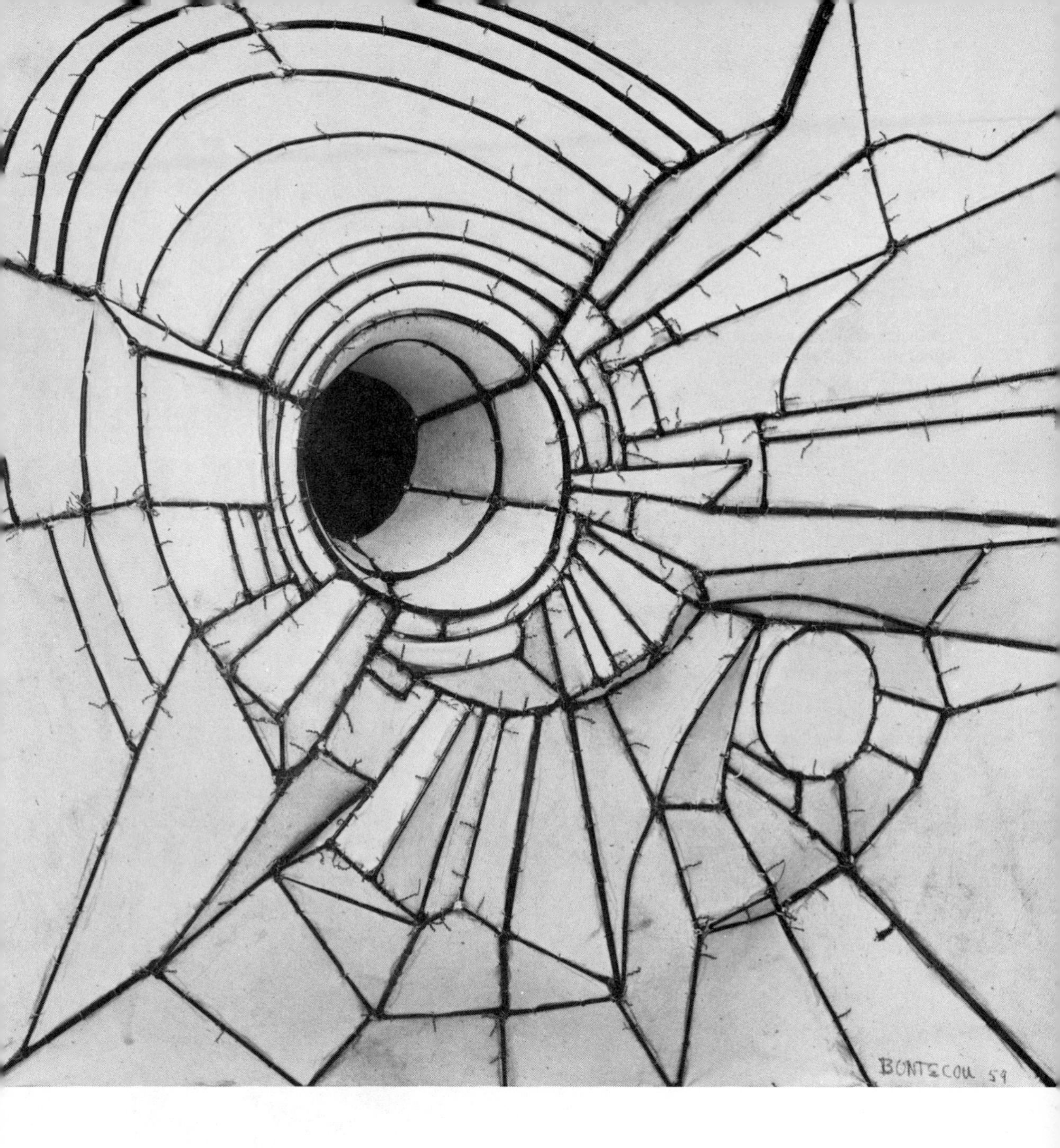

Untitled. Lee Bontecou. 1959. 20⅝″ high, 20⅝″ wide, 7¾″ deep. Canvas and metal. The metal line becomes the structure for attaching the canvas; it emphasizes the shapes contained within. Courtesy, Smith College Museum of Art, Northampton, Massachusetts

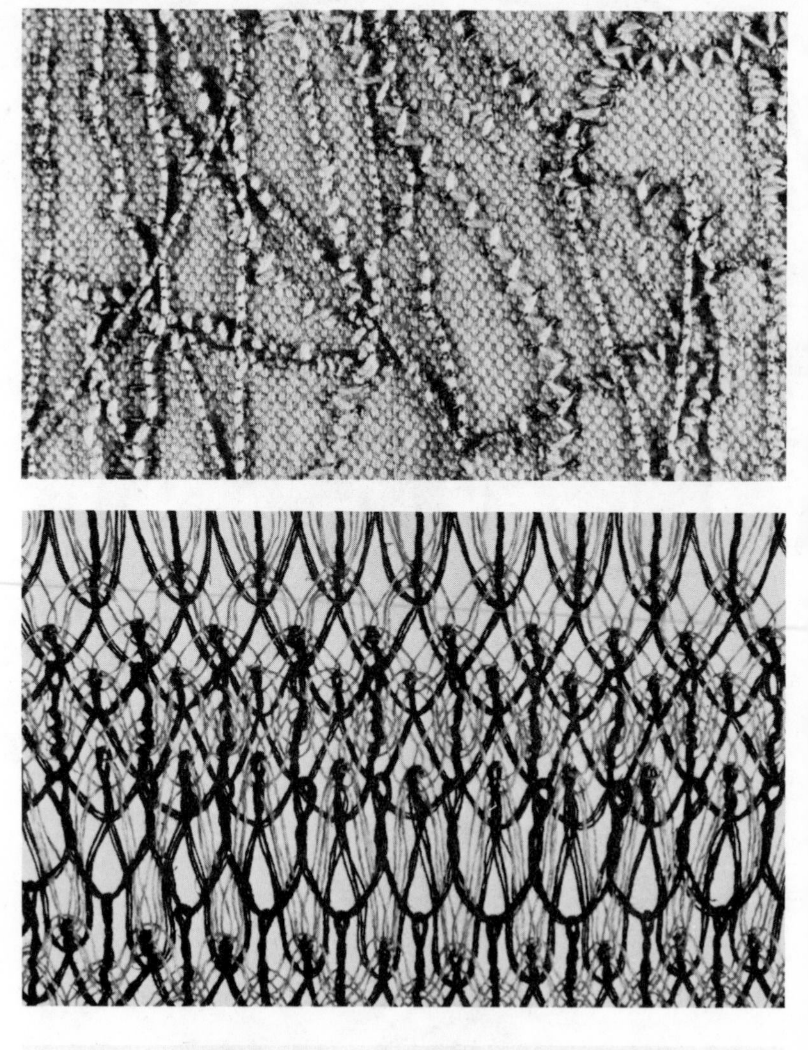

Stepping Stones. (Detail) Blanche Carstenson. Stitchery. The continuous, flowing, straight and zigzag threads have the effect of broken lines because of the sewn threads that fasten them to the backing material.

Open Stream. Evelyn M. Gulick. 27″ high, 19″ wide. The loop and twist of knotless netting combined with needle weaving create an all-over line-pattern repeat. Photo, Harry Crosby

Embroidery. Mariska Karasz. The repetition of embroidered directional lines creates shapes. Diagonal lines, stitched within the leaf shapes, define texture and pattern. Courtesy, The Cooper Union Museum, New York

Winter Window II. (Detail)
Evelyn Svec Ward. 1971. 13½″ high, 25½″ wide. Standing panel. Needlework and knitting. Chenille, maguey, sisal, cotton, wool, linen, mixed threads, and burlap. The various weights of the fibers, and the techniques employed, give variety to the linear quality of the composition. Photo, William E. Ward Collection, Mr. and Mrs. Alan M. Krause

String Composition ⋇70. Sue Fuller. 1956. The medium dictates a composition based on line. Courtesy, The Art Institute of Chicago. Gift, Mr. Emerson Crocker

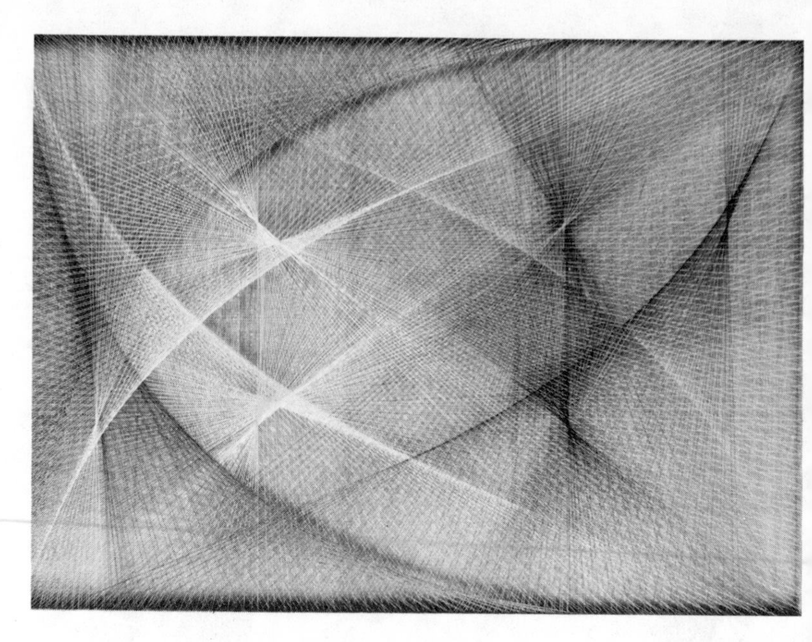

Eight. John Goodyear. 1966. 24¼″ high, 48½″ wide, 8″ deep. Wood, enamel, light, glass. The composition emphasizes an interaction of curved and straight lines using various media. Courtesy, Whitney Museum of American Art, New York

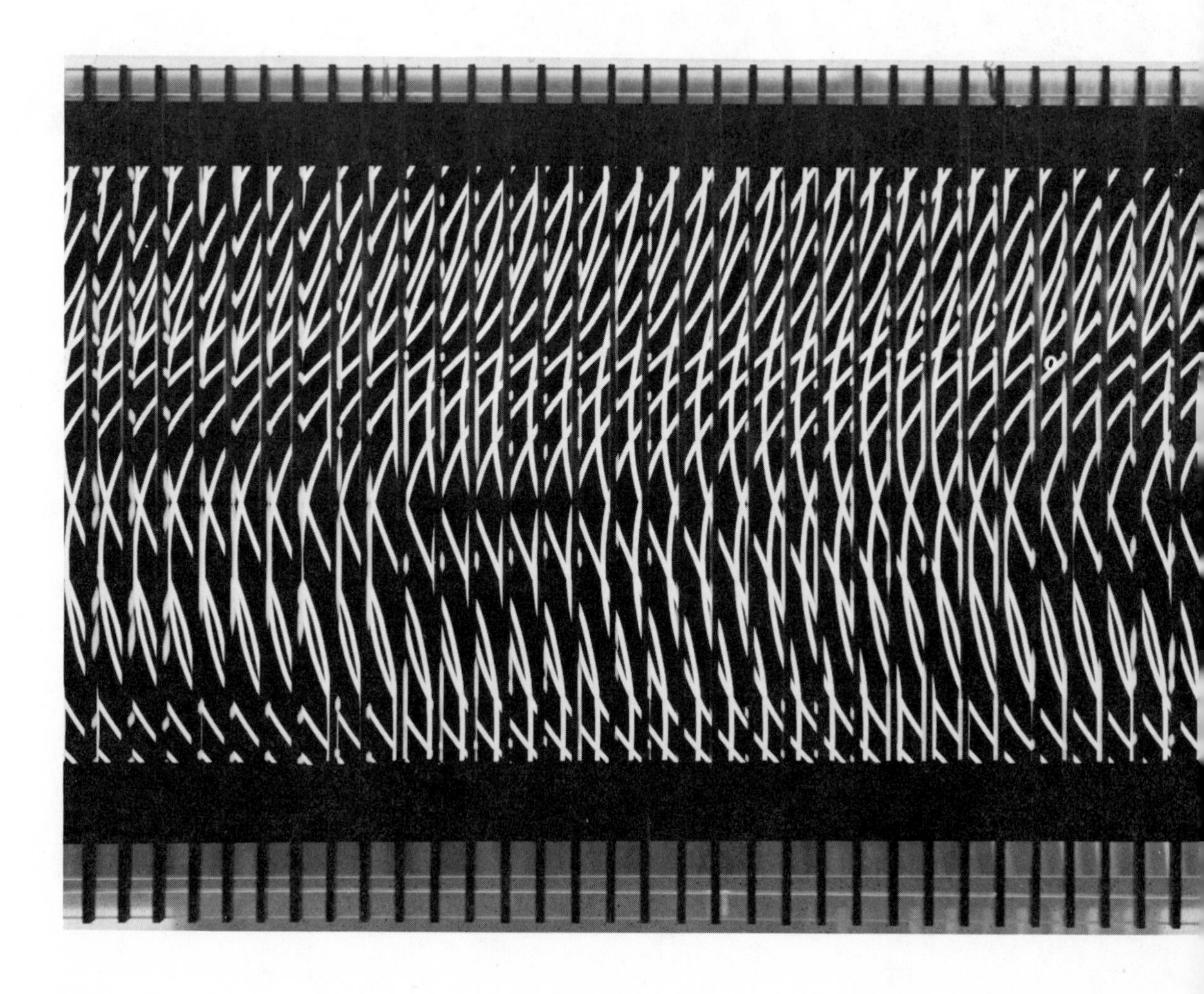

Branch Weaving. Hanna Silver. Structural development relies on the linear interweaving of single threads.

Apache Burden Basket. 11″ high, 19″ diameter. The textural line is evident in the twined construction and design; the narrow, hanging leather strips carry out the linear theme. Collection, Stana Coleman

The Sound of Many Waters. Marianne Childress. 7′ high, 2′ wide. The curved, wrapped linear structure is the support and theme for the entire piece. Free-hanging, decorative strands each form a line. Photo, Ron Garrison

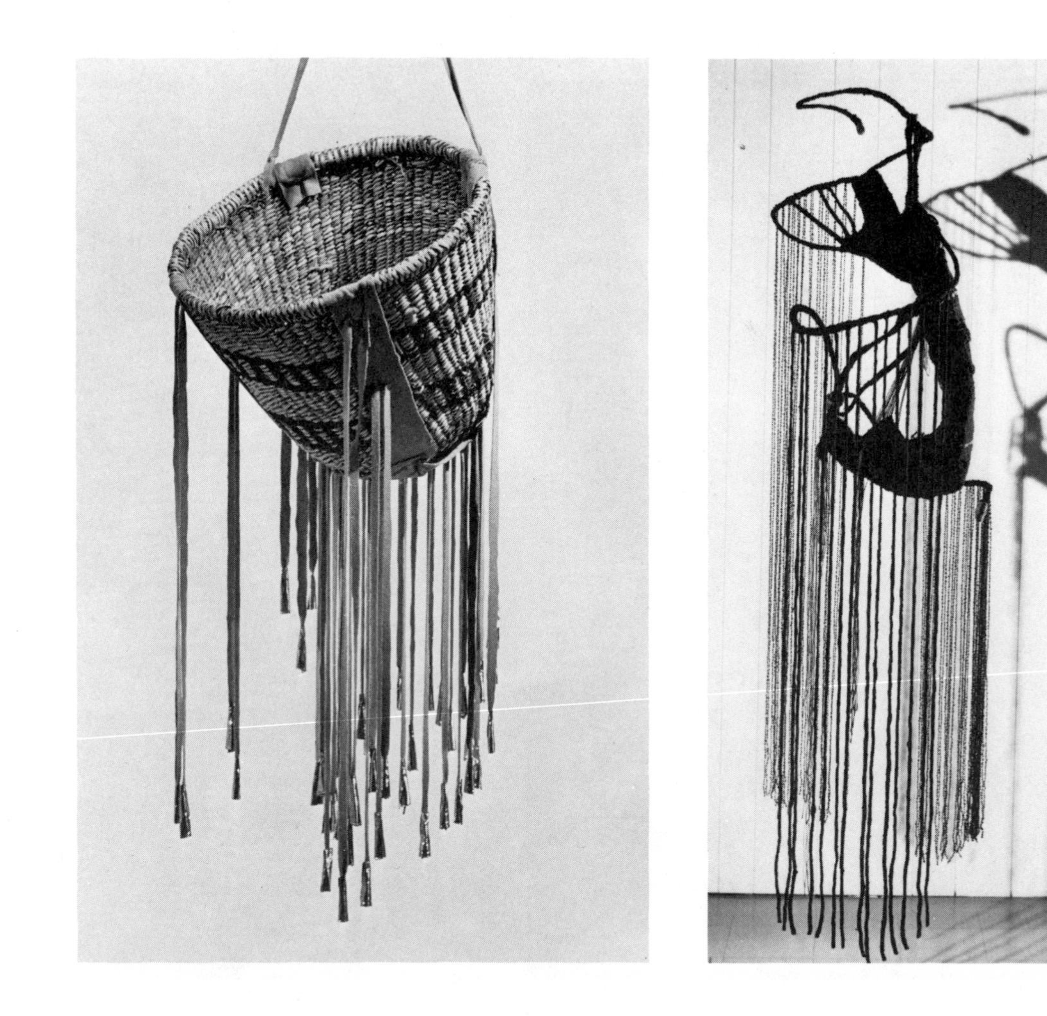

Torso. Harry Kramer. 1964. Wire construction. The wire line defines the form of the torso. Courtesy, Tate Gallery, London

Three Sounds. Tom Kapsalis. Silver soldering. The lines taper toward the outer framework and thicken as they approach the complexity of the central core. Courtesy, artist

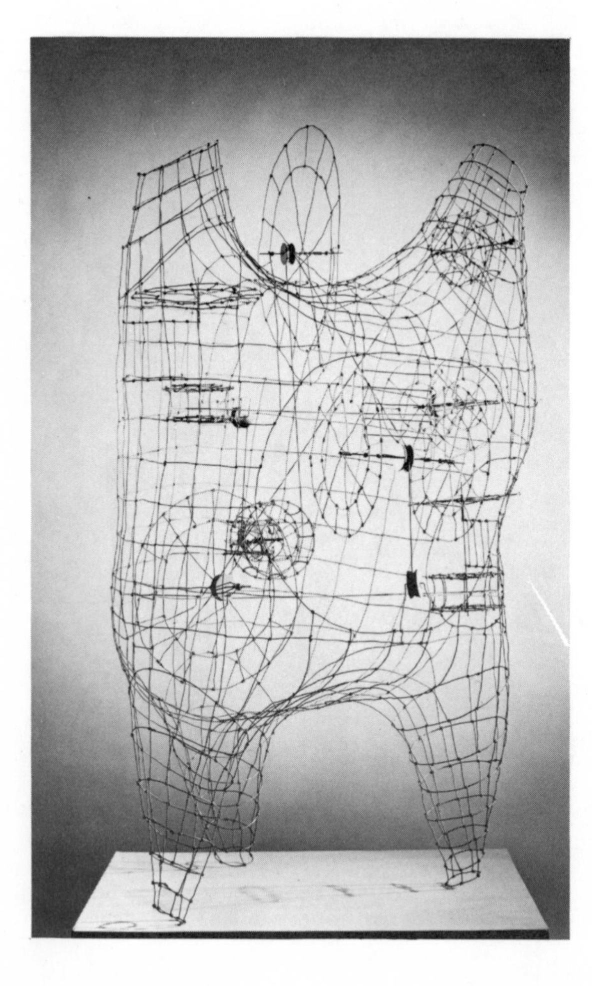

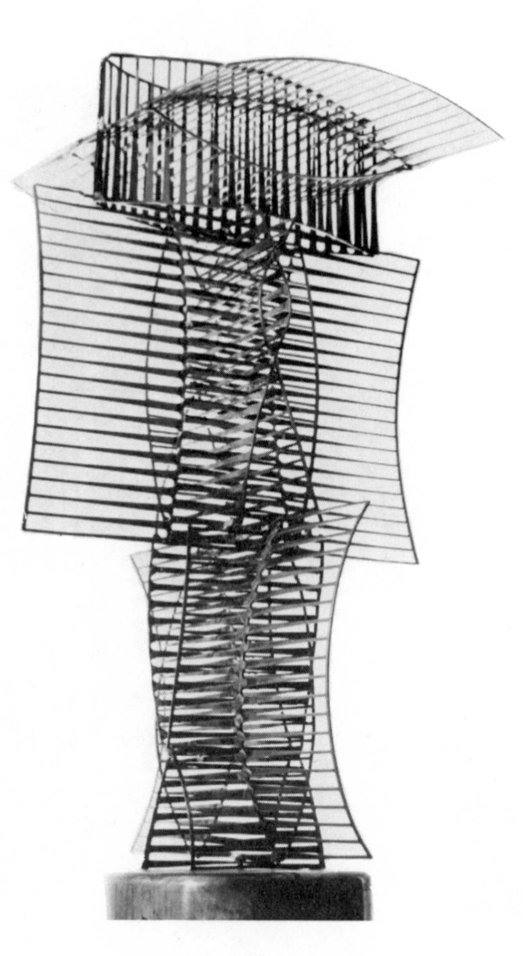

Consciousness. Joan Michaels Paque. Knotting. The technique automatically creates a three-dimensional line that twists around for composition and structure. Photo, Henry Paque

Fiber Sculpture. (Detail) Lee Erlin Snow. Wrapping and knotting are used to build up form and surface treatment as three-dimensional line.

Red Diamond. (Detail) Hildegarde Klene. The macramé and loose, end-knotted strands add a linear element to the hooked-fiber hanging. Photo, J. Bermudez

Night Light Photographs. Jay Hinz. Taken with open camera aperture directed at neon lights from a moving vehicle. The camera provides a tool for seeking lines in the atmosphere and the environment. Notice the variation in line—bold, delicate, blurred, knotted, dotted.

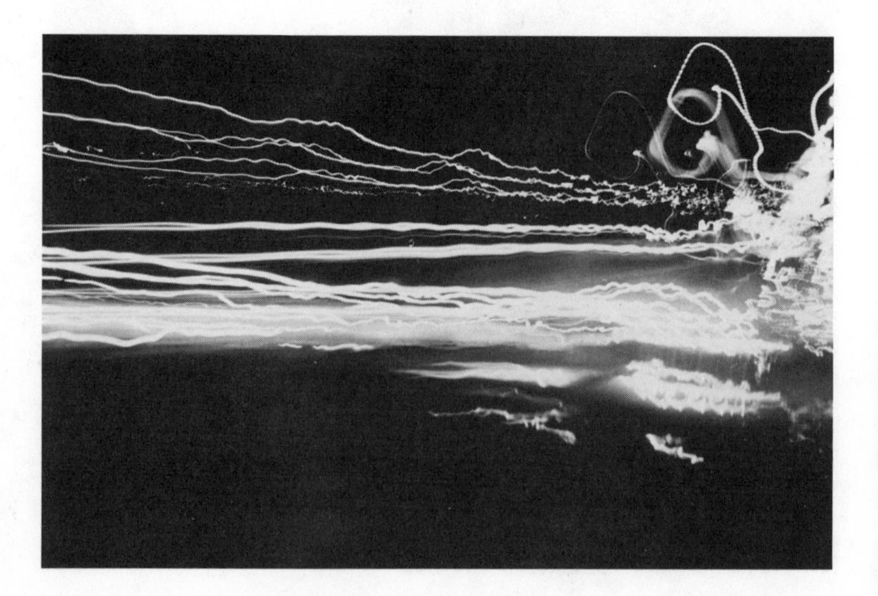

EXERCISES

First, use a sharp medium-lead pencil, then any other drawing tool, to complete the following exercises on 4″× 6″ white paper:

1. Draw one straight, uniformly thick line; draw another thick and thin line. Make each delicate and then bold.
2. Make a series of straight vertical lines from left to right using uniform spacing and random spacing.
3. Make a series of bent lines, twisted lines, wavy lines.
4. Make a series of lines interrupted by forms suggested beneath the surface.
   Begin with a straight, horizontal line. As it travels from left to right, imagine a box or other three-dimensional shape beneath the surface and let the line continue up, around, and down the edges of it to continue again on a horizontal course. The lines and imagined forms can be exactly alike when repeated one on top of the other, or they can be altered to give variety.
5. Starting at the left of the paper, place your pencil on the paper and move your entire arm across the paper without flexing the wrist (arm action).
6. Make a series of vertical strokes, moving just the hand not the arm.
7. Select a natural object such as tree bark, a plank of wood, a leaf, feathers, shells, or a piece of marble. Make a detailed pen-and-ink analysis in line, using contrasting qualities and thicknesses of line—straight, curved, dotted, broken, continuous, delicate, bold, uniform, thick and thin, in different directions in zigzags, angular, perpendicular, horizontal, or vertical.
8. Draw a contour of your hand. First, with your eyes only, decide where you are going to start. Continue to let your eyes trace the outline of your hand. Simultaneously, let your pencil follow the same movement on your paper. Do not take your eyes from your hand; do not look at the paper while you are drawing. Periodically you may check and re-establish your position. Introduce inner structural lines such as those that curve over finger joints, outlines of fingernails, or a ring you may be wearing.
9. Delicately outline your hand and define the dorsal portion of it and each finger by a continuous back and forth curving line to suggest the form beneath. This technique is known as bracelet shading.
10. Make an unbroken line that fills the entire format.

CHAPTER 6

Two-dimensional Shape

A shape is composed of a two-dimensional area having height and width. The shape of an area is one of the most prominent characteristics by which objects may be perceived through the senses. Shape suggests order. If an object cannot be recognized, it is considered to be "shapeless." The shape of an object helps us identify and categorize it for future reference and recognition.

Two-dimensional shape, or form, is a closed figure described by an outline or contour. When this line enclosing space is solidly filled in as a flat plane, it becomes a silhouette and is perceived as a shape. Whenever two areas overlap, a third shape results. Shapes may be divided into two basic categories: (1) natural, and (2) geometric or man-made.

Natural Shapes

The amoeboid shapes used in contemporary design have counterparts in nature. Morphological similarities are apparent in microscopic forms, fungi, rocks, roots, atmospheric formations, and water patterns. The shapes in nature are often free form, amoeboid, ever-changing. Proportion and rhythm are revealed as indigenous to growth as, for example, in the repetitions of a tree's growth rings. Since nature is involved with living organisms, growth is integrally bound up with it and its dynamic structure. The division of living cells occurs in geometric progression and prepares for a specialization of function. This causes a greater division of cells in one direction and a slowing of growth in another, producing asymmetrical patterning. In such cases, the structures of the cells are changed for the functional purpose of adapting them for their role in life.

Fish. Jay Hinz. Black-and-white construction paper design. Negative photostat. Two-dimensional shape and line; several dot accents.

Ready to Wear. Stuart Davis. 1955. 56¼″ high, 42″ wide. Oil. Courtesy, The Art Institute of Chicago. Sigmund W. Kunstadler Gift and Goodman Fund

Aesthetically, these same growth processes may be utilized in designing. A shape may be repeated uniformly. Then via subtle transition, the shape may begin to change. This change can be brought about through alteration of the shape itself, its size, the regularity of its repetition, or the angle of its position within the design. Continuous rhythmic repetition, periodic repetition, or a regular alternation of one or more forms may provide a patterning that provides an over-all new form. A solitary shape may be altered slightly with each repetition or it may regularly vary in length, weight, or position.

Our world is composed of a seemingly limitless variety of shapes. However, certain basic shapes help reduce this variety to simplicity and order. Proportion and rhythm, which are principles of design, are characteristics of natural form. Differences in the proportion and the arrangement of the same scientific elements make up our world. Rhythm is programmed recurrence. The multiplicity of a form, or a shape, becomes a variation on a theme and results in the unity of the whole.

Sylvette Bleue-Violette. Pablo Picasso. 1954. 51⅜″ high, 38⅛″ wide. Oil on canvas. Courtesy, The Art Institute of Chicago. Gift, Mr. & Mrs. Leigh B. Block

The undulating, flowing forms of nature may be taut, triggered to sprout yet another form, smaller in scale, but in exact duplication of its original shape. Or it may burst forth from its seed capsule in a variety of ways. The resulting shapes will reflect the movement of unfurling, radiating, pointing, dispersing, and disintegrating which occur within one life cycle. These shapes cover the extremes from the most delicately precise to the totally indefinite, from the pinched new growth to the decayed disintegration of the death form.

Shapes in nature occur in different scales. Some of these shapes may be seen with the naked eye. Others may be seen only when magnified. Microphotographs of natural elements, as well as products of electronic science, provide lucrative sources of inspiration for the reinterpretation of shape.

Repeated shapes create a pattern, such as a honeycomb. The total structure may be quite different from that of each unit shape which makes it up. Certain shapes recur frequently in natural objects, but the variations are innu-

The Priests. Ralph Arnold. Linoleum-block print. Flat pattern in only black and white. Collection, Dona Meilach

Notebook Sketch. Bill Hinz. Ink marker. In a simple drawing, a harmony is achieved by repeating shapes and lines.

merable. Non-objective shapes applied to design suggest forms derived from nature; they do not necessarily identify with recognizable objects.

Geometric and Man-made Shapes

Geometric shapes reflect the environment of man. Geometric segments are seen in buildings, machines, and in the many objects which fulfill our everyday needs. Geometric two-dimensional areas are either squares, rectangles, circles, ellipses, triangles, rhomboids, trapezoids, trapeziums, pentagons, hexagons, heptagons, octagons, or irregular polygons. Most objects may be reduced to simple geometrics. This simplification process is known as abstraction. For example, a building may become a series of squares, rectangles, triangles, or a combination thereof.

The structure of art is composed from both regularly and irregularly spaced units or shapes. They may combine to form other structures. We can invent shapes by the restructuring of the familiar. We can create different, exciting shapes by using our powers of observation and imagination.

Accidental circumstances such as a cast shadow, an ink blot, or a pattern of cracks in old paint may provide the potential for a similarly inspired shape. Shapes that pique the imagination may be found everywhere—in a crumpled sheet of paper, a random grouping of pebbles, feathers on a duck's back, the strata of rocks, the bark of a tree.

Kids and Kat. Bill Hinz. Sketchbook ink drawing illustrates the beginning and general development of a two-dimensional theme.

Another possibility exists in the spiral that builds in size by progressive repetition of its own basic shape.

The designer should develop the ability to recognize potential inspiration that exists all around. The selectivity we exercise when we choose and rearrange "chance" shapes into a new form strengthens our sensitivity. We may transform and refine shapes by simplification, change of scale, and the addition to, or removal of, portions of the original shape. Shapes may be divided or multiplied. All of these alterations will result in "new" forms.

Figure/ground relationships are shape/space relationships. The figure is usually perceived as on top of, or in front of, the ground. Sometimes it makes holes in it. The ground may be either perceived as a surface or as a space. We ordinarily consider the shape of the figure. However, ground areas also have form, that is, the negative form of remaining space. Both positive and negative shapes and spaces are important in designing. Used together, they complement one another. When cutting out shapes, negative shapes may be combined with positive shapes to create a "new" combined form.

To experiment with this concept, cut out a shape (A) from a piece of black paper, but do not destroy the piece (B) from which it was cut. Position the cut-out shape (A) on a background of white paper. Crop the edges of the piece (B) to a complementary outer shape, and then superimpose it on the first shape (A). The duplication of the

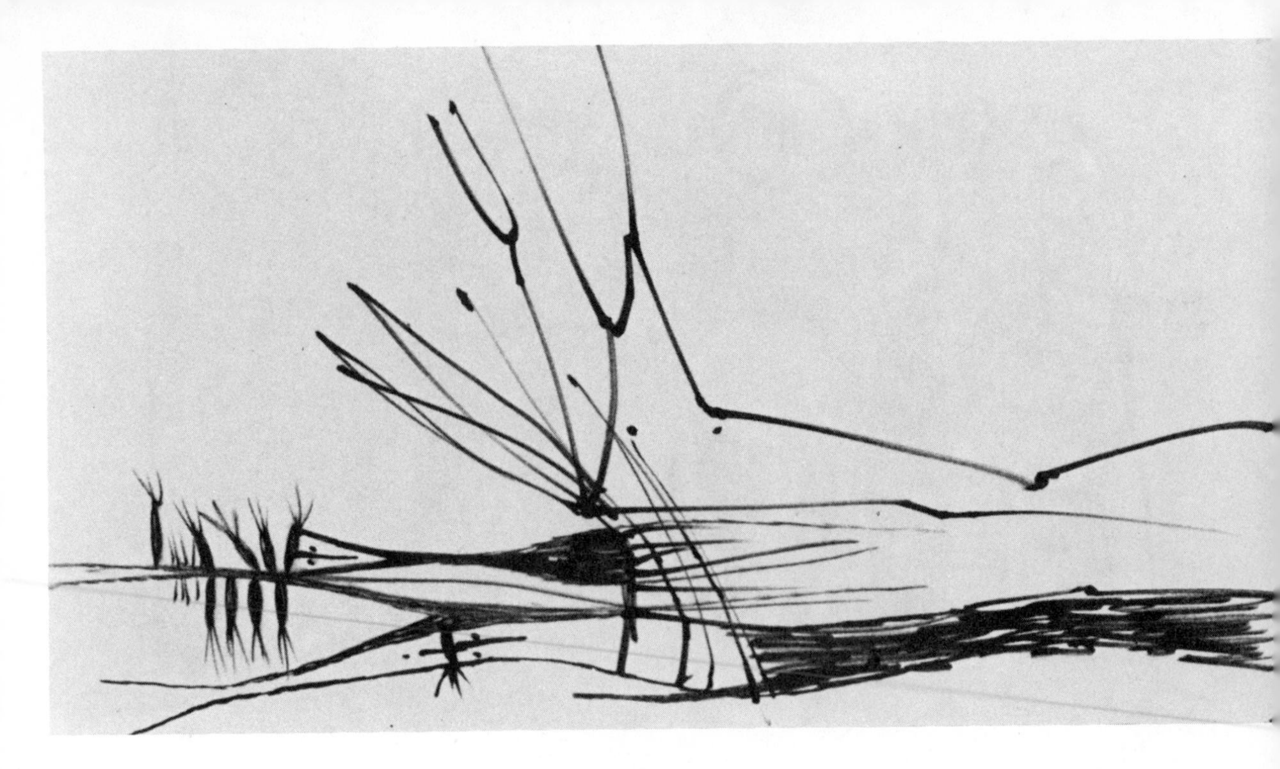

Notebook Sketch. Bill Hinz.

⋇98 Shinto Shrine. Ann Roman. Paper collage. Two-dimensional shapes can be developed in many media.

Collage. Dona Meilach. Two-dimensional geometric shapes based on repetition of different-sized squares and rectangles.

Takamashi. Robert Borchard. Serigraph.

Medieval Images. Robert Borchard. Serigraph.

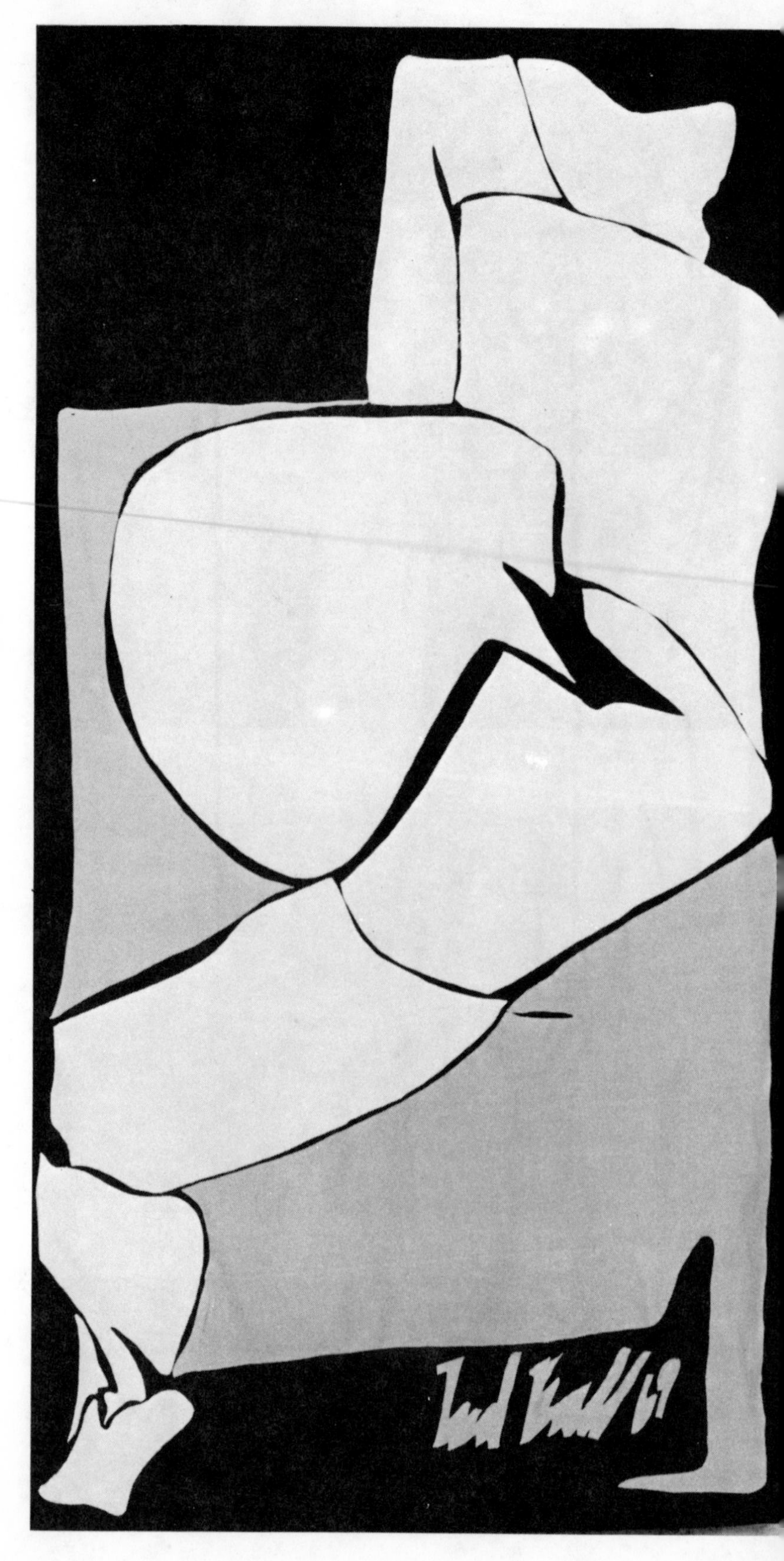

Nude. Ted Ball. 1969. Simple, massive two-dimensional shapes convey the subject. Photo, Bob Lopez

Storm. (Detail) Evelyn Lewy. Collagraph.

Storm. Evelyn Lewy. Collagraph. Collection, Lee Erlin Snow

Non-woven Weaving. (Opposite) Rochelle Myers. 1972. 48″ high, 30″ wide. Fabrics, hand-painted papers, plastic tapes. A symmetrical pattern is relieved by the variation of compatible shapes within the central panel. Courtesy, artist

Mola. San Blas Indians. Fabric appliqué. Repetition of different colors and sizes creates harmony and pattern.

The Old Piano. Elvie Ten Hoor. Collage. Two-dimensional suede and leather shapes. Both sides of the material are used for different textural effects.

Composition No. 3. Julian Martin de Vidales. 1970. Tooled-leather mural exhibits simple two-dimensional shapes. Detailed linear and textural tooling adds contrast within the darker value areas. Courtesy, Galeria Juana Mordo, Madrid

Granada ⁂2. Claude Bentley. 39½″ square. Assemblage of flat wood shapes on canvas.

Sketchbook Drawing. Bill Hinz. A quick-idea sketch for a two-dimensional design.

two shapes will result in a close harmony. The value contrasts and the care taken in the arranging of these pieces prevent the sameness of the two shapes from becoming monotonous.

When similar elements are joined, as above, unpredictable shapes occur which create interest and repetition of the combined similar elements. The way in which the connected units are placed and the number of repetitions contribute to the uniqueness of the new shape. The negative and positive shapes may assume equal importance, or one or the other may create a dominance in the composition.

The principle of balance is integrally associated with shape. Balance suggests a weighing scale. Mirror-image shapes placed on either side of a central line create a symmetrical or axial balance. One or more shapes positioned on either side of a central line may be different but equal in weight. A sense of balance is achieved by the thoughtful positioning of similar forms. Radial-balanced objects jutting out from a common central core reflect symmetrical balance. One shape may be slightly altered with each, or any, repetition or be repeated with periodic changes in size.

EXERCISES

Within a 6″ square of white paper, use only vertical pencil strokes, and no outlines, to create a two-dimensional design in values of black, white, and gray in the following ways:

1 Use squares and rectangles. You may use squares and rectangles within each other, but do not have a portion of a shape overlapping an edge.

2 Use squares and rectangles whose shapes have been slightly altered, for example, with rounded corners.

3 Divide the 6″ square into three equal or unequal basic shapes, one each of black, white, and gray. These three shapes may be outlined by lines that are curvilinear, amoeboid, rectilinear, or combinations of these. The lines must contact an edge of the format on either end. Introduce black and gray shapes into the white shape, black and white shapes into the gray shape, and gray and white shapes into the black shape to integrate them and bring them into closer harmony.

4 Place tracing paper over the last three designs and create a line pattern for each. There should be something in common between the line and the shapes.

5 Divide a 6″ square by using three curved lines, both ends of which must contact an edge of the format or contact another line. (There should be no free-dangling lines.) Use balanced black, white, and gray in filling in the shapes between the lines.

- A. Select black and white magazine-type faces (letters) and cut them apart into groups of three horizontal lines of type. Separate these groups into piles of light, middle, and dark values.
- B. Establish the rhythm you wish to maintain, such as following the curve of an edge, and lay in your strips of letters as in a mosaic. Glue down.
- C. Maintain the value pattern of your original sketch. Keep the value consistent within a shape by the selection of the appropriate type groups.

6 Using a tree as inspiration, create shapes that suggest a tree with its inner branching structure, to break up a 2″×6″ rectangle. Add a harmonious line pattern. Use value reversals (black on white and white on black for extreme contrast) and gray areas for transition.

7 Use three sizes of squares, rectangles, and triangles in black, white, and gray to create a pattern of chimneys.

Chintil a Spiru. Sylone. 1964. Woven tapestry.

CHAPTER 7

Three-dimensional Design

Blanchet Doors. Mabel Hutchinson. 6′ 8″ high, 6′ wide. The design theme was set by two wood pieces forming an arch at the top. From this dominant line, she worked to achieve a harmonious rhythm throughout. Courtesy, artist

In two-dimensional media, such as painting and printmaking, illusions of depth, perspective, and space are created by drawing and graduated values. The result is a symbolic representation of solid volumes actually existing in space. The viewer imagines that the objects seen in the painting could also be seen from the opposite side. However, he knows this is not possible and that this illusion has been painted on a two-dimensional plane.

An interim dimension exists between the second and the third dimension. This is known as "bas-relief" or "low relief." Foreground shapes, or figures, project outward from a continuous background plane. Although the bas-relief has the third dimension of depth, this depth is shallow; it does not include the back of the carving and, therefore, does not produce sculpture-in-the-round. An early known example of this low-relief sculpture is the Parthenon frieze. The sculptured forms produce a constantly changing interplay of light and shadow created by the dimension of partial depth.

When the real third dimension of depth is added to the two dimensions of length and width, the result is a volume, or mass, which is the three-dimensional counterpart of shape. It occupies space and is concerned with shape, size, depth, and weight. When a shape becomes three-dimensional, its volume is usually perceived as constant in shape. We would have to walk around it to avoid bumping into it.

A volume can represent different things. It can be a solid, enclosed, weighty mass or an open, spatial structure.

Drift. Irwin Gwyther. 1967. 36″ high, 48″ wide. Relief construction. Balsawood on blockboard. Overlapping of planes creates a shallow sculptural relief. Courtesy, Gimpel Fils Gallery, London

It can be an empty or negative space or an implied volume created by rapidly rotating planes. A volume can be in static balance weighted down by gravity, or it can float weightlessly in space.

Volume, as one of the basic mass/space elements, can be varied by changing its size, shape, position, direction, number, interval, and density. The solid volumetric shapes

Cosmos. Yasuo Mizui. 1970. Concrete relief façade. No two panels are the same. Courtesy, artist

include the cube, cone, cylinder, sphere, ovoid, pyramid, prism, tetrahedron, octahedron, hexahedron, dodecahedron, and icosahedron. These basic structures can be endlessly elaborated upon in the combination and recombination of their forms. The possibility of creative restructuring was thoroughly discussed in Chapter 6, "Two-dimensional Shape."

Hallelujah. Clyde Burt. Ceramic sculptural relief wall hanging. Separate pieces fit together as a mosaic. The projected depths of the sculptured faces contrast with the flat areas of the arms and hands. Courtesy, artist

Pomona. L. Stanley Carpenter. Wood mosaic relief. Photo, Richard Gross

Fountain-Medical Center. Rhoda LeBlanc Lopez. Ceramic sculptural relief, rich in textural surface treatment, using mainly raised and incised lines and dots. Photo, Curt Breedlove

Big Rubber Lady. Eldon Danhausen. Approximately 40″ diameter. Sculpture-in-the-round fulfills the entire global structure.

Designing for Three Dimensions

Volume, or mass, is the most critical single element in sculpture. It is equally important in other structural design such as architecture, ceramics, glass, and jewelry. An essential criterion to apply when designing for a three-dimensional work is that every side must be well-designed as a unit unto itself as well as designed into the whole as a harmonious modular unit. Every viewing angle is important and must be equally considered. The entire sculpture must present itself as a complete entity. Even when the designer's intent is to have the piece viewed from a particular side, each side must be equally well thought out so as to be aesthetically pleasing.

The general character of a sculpture should pervade throughout. For example, if the piece were rotund and composed of various curvilinear indentations, it would be necessary to carry these indentations carefully around the

Sphere-shaped Pot. Clyde Burt. The repetition of circles on the surface echoes the spherical form. Symmetrical balance is achieved by equal negative and positive areas of natural brown clay body contrasted with the matte charcoal-gray glaze. Courtesy, artist

sphere, breaking into them here and there, as subject and whimsy should dictate, to avoid monotony. However, the viewer's eye should be able to carry the lines invisibly through the interrupted form to complete their continuity. The use of curved lines plays up the roundness of the three-dimensional form. Straight, angular lines would have been contrary to the bulbous quality and would have detracted from the total impact of the piece.

The surface treatment of a piece is another area to be considered in three-dimensional designing. Often, in a sculptured work, the texture of the medium—wood, marble or metal—might dictate how the surface will remain. Gouge marks that might result from the use of the roughing-in tools may be allowed to remain as a surface texture. When metal is used, a natural patina may be desired and planned for in the original design of the piece. The color will be

Folded Paper. Dona Meilach. Symmetrical repeat pattern in relief, purposely designed to pick up shadow patterns. Paper design can be interpreted in ceramics, concrete, and other hard materials.

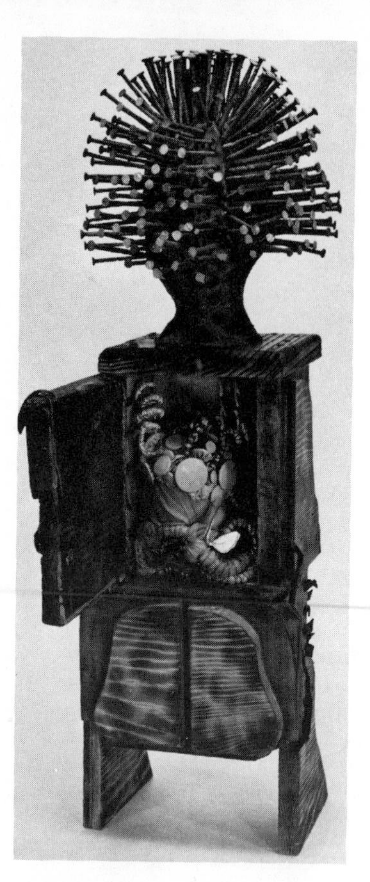

Fetish Sculpture. Irene Salava. Wood, metal, leather, mirror, and batiked stuffed fabric. The sculpture-in-the-round emphasizes negative space and several compartments that open and shut with the interiors carefully composed of assembled parts.

Bather. (Detail) Irene Salava. Wood, metal, feathers, fake fur, fabric, rope, acrylic paint. The head portion shows negative and positive space, assemblage and drawing.

altered greatly through the natural weathering process. Sometimes, this may be hastened along by chemical treatment. Other surface embellishments may be planned as linear or textural additions or carving. In some cases, the designer may choose to add a painted design. For the ceramist, a repeat pattern may be painted over the entire clay surface with a liquid-rubber resist and the object then dipped into glaze. The resist is peeled off after the color has partially dried.

Whatever the method of surface enhancement, one thing above all else is important. The design should become "one" with the form. The form and material should suggest the direction of its surface treatment. If the form is fluid, the surface design should echo fluidity. If the form is stark and angular, the surface patterning should follow the same feeling.

Untitled. Julius Schmidt. 1961. 21½″ high. Iron. An interesting adaptation of a cylindrical form, utilizing sculptural line and dot. Courtesy, Marlborough-Gerson Gallery, Inc., New York

Paper Sculpture. James Higa. (An enlarged detail.) The entire structure (right) is built up of repeated disk-based forms of crimped newspaper assembled in a staggered arrangement. Photos, Mel Meilach

Cosmic Man. (Opposite) Peter Boiger. 1971. Metal. The top section is an inverted, smaller-scaled repeat of the lower form. The texture and interior ribs add to the total interest. Courtesy, artist

Untitled. Roger Kotoske. 1970. The distortion of the reflected images adds to the dimension of the polyester-resin transparent sculpture. Courtesy, artist

Reclining Figure. Henry Moore. Wood. The wood sculpture capitalized on recessed areas, negative space, natural grain, and the sculptured rounded form. Courtesy, artist

Song. Philip Grausman. 1968. 11½″ high, 21″ wide, 11½″ deep. Marble. Shapes and shadows form an ever-changing interplay. Courtesy, Grace Borgenicht Gallery, Inc., New York

Planter. Rhoda LeBlanc Lopez. 27″ high. Brown clay, reduced. The surface design conforms and relates to the curve of the pot structure. Observe the contour similarity in the two portions, but they are executed with different elements dominating. Courtesy, artist

Pot. Carol Bloomberg. A ceramic pot suggests an organic structure. Changing textures are repeated in the sphere and in the base for unity, harmony, etc. Courtesy, artist

Untitled. Jane Knight. Sculpture in knitted fibers with braided and free-hanging cords for a linear element. Photo, Richard Knight

Untitled. Park Chambers. Freestanding floor sculpture, emphasizing contrasting values and textures with fibers. Courtesy, artist

Snail. Berni Gorski. 20″ long, 13½″ high, 5″ wide. Antique silk, stitchery, beads, and knitting are creatively used for a stuffed fabric sculpture. Courtesy, artist

Primitive Mask. Ambrym Island, New Hebrides. Hemp fibers, bark, traces of color are artistically designed by a primitive craftsman and can provide stimulus for modern design and materials to use for sculpture. Courtesy, The Art Institute of Chicago

Sisal Basket. Kathryn McCardle. Clove-hitched macramé. The sisal-cord structural coil and frayed top adornment, with contrasting values in the twisting forms, combine in a unique fiber statement.

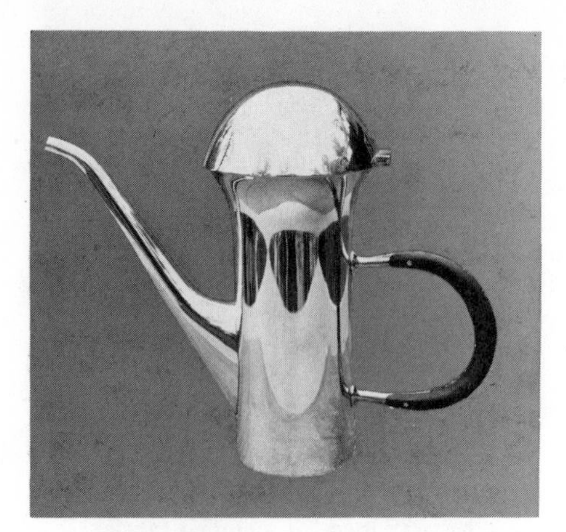

Silver Serving Pot. Judith and Humphrey Gilbert. The clean-cut lines of the form repeat in the curves of the spout, lid, and handle. Courtesy, artist

Monoangulated Surface in Space. Max Bill. The sculpture relies on its elegance of form and material. Courtesy, Detroit Institute of Arts, Detroit, Michigan

The Shell. Thea Tewi. 36″ wide, 23″ high, 18″ deep. Green Vermont marble. The beauty of the marble grain is emphasized by the form repeating its curve. Photo, O. E. Nelson Courtesy, La Boetie, Inc.

EXERCISES

The following problems deal with space occupied by three-dimensional volume.

1 *Sculpture: Additive*

Materials that can be manipulated or joined to form an object in space (paper, wood, found objects, clay, plaster, stone, concrete, plastic, and welded metal).

Make a voodoo rattle.

A. Select a balloon shape. Blow it up to the desired size. Tie a secure knot in the end. Grease the balloon with vaseline and do either of the following:

1. Cover the balloon with several layers of thin strips of gauze soaked in watered-down white glue. If a thin shell is created, light will show through, creating a transparent effect.
2. Cover the balloon with at least three layers of papier-mache strips (or paper-pulp mache). To differentiate between the layers of mache, use colored strips from the comic pages for the second layer.

B. Deflate the balloon with a pin and remove. Pour seeds or small stones into the hole to create the rattle. A cardboard tube from a cleaners' hanger could be inserted and glued into the end from which the balloon is removed. Sand the final layer smooth with fine-grained sandpaper.

C. Paint the surface of your rattle with a primitive geometric design in earth colors of black, red-brown, yellow-ocher, and white. Look up the primitive designs of different cultures.

2 *Sculpture: Subtractive*

Materials that can be shaped or cut away from a solid mass, such as stone (marble, limestone, sandstone, basalt), wood, plaster, or plastic.

To help you begin thinking three-dimensionally: Construct a geometric paper sculpture by scoring and folding the paper and clipping and gluing where necessary to maintain the desired form. Then interpret the paper sculpture in the subtractive method.

A. Pour a block of plaster. Carve portions away to duplicate the angles of the paper sculpture.

B. Use a block of plasticene clay and interpret the angles into your own design.

Feast Bowl. Height of head, 12½″. Wood, carved, Kwakiutl, nineteenth century A.D. Vancouver Island, British Columbia. Sculptural relief, convex and concave positive shapes, and negative spaces define the head. Photo, Field Museum of Natural History, Chicago

Cherry Chair. Hal E. Davis. The shape of the back of the chair is echoed in the joining of the various sections of wood that make up its structure. Courtesy, artist

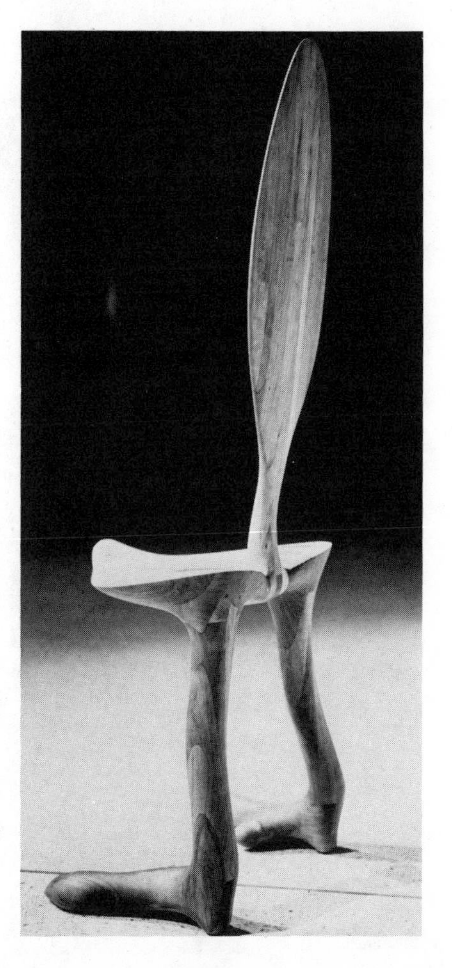

CHAPTER 8

Texture

The word "texture" refers to the surface quality of a substance. Everything has its own characteristic texture. Texture provides man with a means of exploring his environment through his senses. Information about surface textures is gained from our senses of touch and sight. When it is impossible for us actually to experience touching a surface, for example, a moon crater, we must rely on the information our eyes give us as to the properties of that surface. The visual textures must substitute for the tactile experience.

Our eyes share in the discovery of uniqueness in every tactile sensation we experience. A wooden surface looks and feels smooth or rough-grained, pitted or pocked. A smooth surface and a continuous plane of one uninterrupted value are free from shadow except when they have reflective properties such as satin or stainless steel. A striated surface would create ridges of light and shadow.

The perceptual differences in visual textures are caused by variations in the reflection and absorption of light by different materials in varying degrees. Differences in value result from the reaction of light to the diffractive, diffusive, and opaque properties of surface mutations. Differences in color are caused by the selective absorption and reflection of the various wavelengths in light. Differences in the properties of opacity, translucency, or transparency of a material are caused by the varying depths throughout the surface at which the absorption and reflection of light occur.

The scale or size of a form determines whether it is a form or a textural component. If a pebble, for example, is viewed at close range, its contour will inform us of its

Peeling Paint. The textural pattern contains such elements as dot, line, two-dimensional shape, negative and positive space, three-dimensional form and value; it involves the principles of repetition, variety, rhythm, harmony, and unity.

Chipped Paint. The variety of scale, value pattern, and the position of the lifting paint chips are a marvelous inspiration for texture in a design.

shape, but if it is brought closer, the surface pitting and pocking becomes more prevalent and we become more aware of its *textural* surface.

Variations of light and dark create visual texture. *Variation* relieves the monotony of "sameness."

When you use textures in a design, the same consideration must be given to its placement and repetition as with any of the other elements. It is wise to limit the number of textures used within one design so that it will not become too busy. Textural areas provide middle value areas in a design and serve as a transition between the black areas and the white areas. When textures are translated into color, middle-value colors replace the gray, dark colors replace black, and light colors replace white. Subtle textural effects may be achieved by introducing textures in the same value or in a lighter value than the ground to which it is to be applied.

Texture can result from materials, tools, and techniques. As the designer, you must select and separate textures into the two categories: tactile and visual. If it is to be tactile, the "real" texture must be present—feathers and wool in a

Reclining Figure. Henry Moore. 1957–58. Roman travertine marble has a natural texture that becomes an over-all design in the form. Collection, UNESCO Building, Paris

macramé wall hanging, nailheads in a box relief, travertine marble in a sculptured figure. Other textural effects may be created by the manipulation of the materials. A wood plank cut at an angle will guarantee patterning in the grain. Looped fibers will present a texture different from clipped, knotted, crocheted, braided, or wrapped fibers. Gouge marks of a single tool will make a rhythmical pattern and produce its own texture. The pattern in which bricks are laid and the angle in which they are viewed can create textural variety. Metal pieces identical in shape, repeated, overlapped, and interspersed with nailheads, can produce their own texture. Embroidery stitches of many varieties and lengths suggest other textural surface possibilities. Certain glazes applied to clay bodies produce crazing or pitting. Pigment enhances the textural surface of a painting. A palette knife will create a texture different from that of a brush.

As the designer, you select the textural patterns that will best suit your design. You may repeat the same texture, alter it slightly or add another texture which will harmonize with the first. Examples are offered to provide the impetus for creativity. Improvisations on one theme are infinite.

Whalebone Comb. Polynesia–New Zealand. The inherent texture of the whalebone is a random dot. Courtesy, Field Museum of Natural History, Chicago

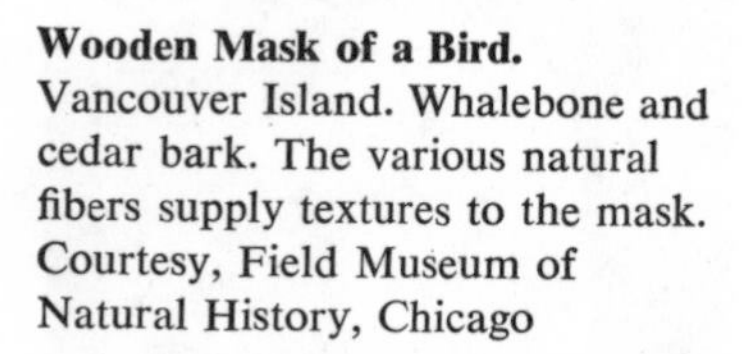

Wooden Mask of a Bird. Vancouver Island. Whalebone and cedar bark. The various natural fibers supply textures to the mask. Courtesy, Field Museum of Natural History, Chicago

Bracteates. Gotland Hemse Kodings. Gold, decorated, eighth century A.D. The concentric patterning of the texture conforms to the circular shape it embellishes. Courtesy, The Art Institute of Chicago

Not Wanted. (Detail) George Buehr. Collage. The fingerprint texture is one we are all familiar with; the subtle face behind provides a surprise photographic dot texture. Photo, Nickerson

Lunar Landscape from Apollo 11. Harve Schaefer. 24″ circle. Textural collage. All varieties of nailheads used for texture relate to the rounded form. Courtesy, artist

Haida Moon Crest. (Detail of left half) Wood. The carver followed the grain of the wood which provides the texture and movement. Photo, Field Museum of Natural History, Chicago

Macramé and Feathers. (Detail) Leora K. Stewart. The fluffy natural texture of the feathers contrasts with the knotting pattern texture. Courtesy, artist

Hooking and Macramé. (Detail) Lorraine Ohlson. The textures are a natural outgrowth of the techniques and materials used.

Woven Hanging. (Detail) The contrasts in texture result from the weave patterns and different fiber.

American Fetish I. (Detail) Lee Erlin Snow. Crochet, braiding, and wrapping using hard- and soft-finish cords.

Rya Pillow. (Detail) Bill Hinz. The same linear yarn texture prevails throughout. The only variation exists in the height of the pile. The lower pile is more compact, producing a change in the visual texture.

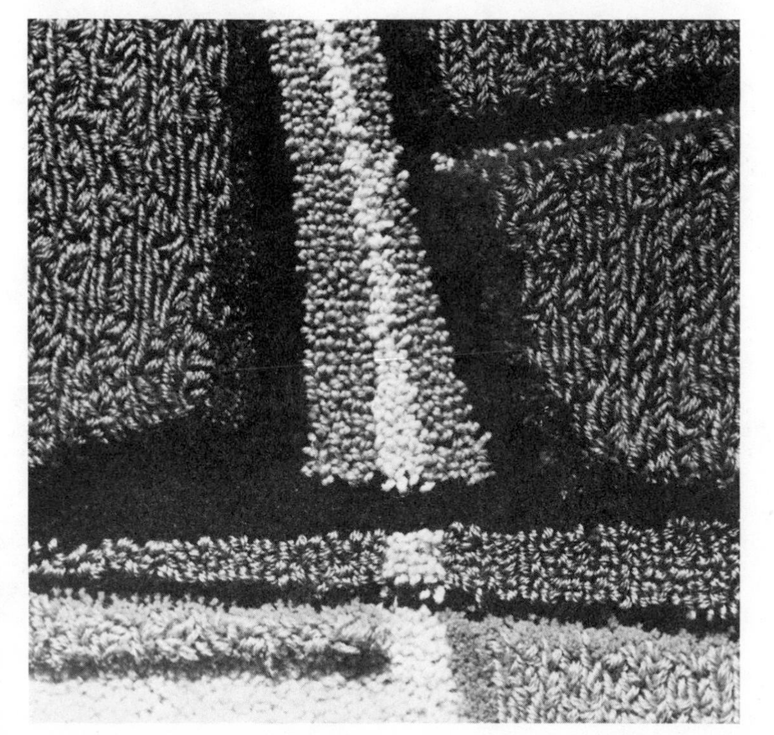

Hooked Wall Hanging. (Detail) Bill Hinz. Wool. The types of yarns and the heights of pile determine the textural variation.

Brick Passageway. The texture is developed through the stagger-repeat pattern of the protruding bricks, alternated with the flush-laid brick columns. Photo, Mel Meilach

Petit Soir le Matin. Zoltan Kemeny. 1959. 35⅝″ high, 39⅝″ wide. Aluminum and brass. The edges of the layered and bent thin sheets of metal provide a horizontal linear texture. Nailheads provide several textures, determined by their grouping or positioning. Courtesy, The Art Institute of Chicago Collection, Wirt D. Walker Fund

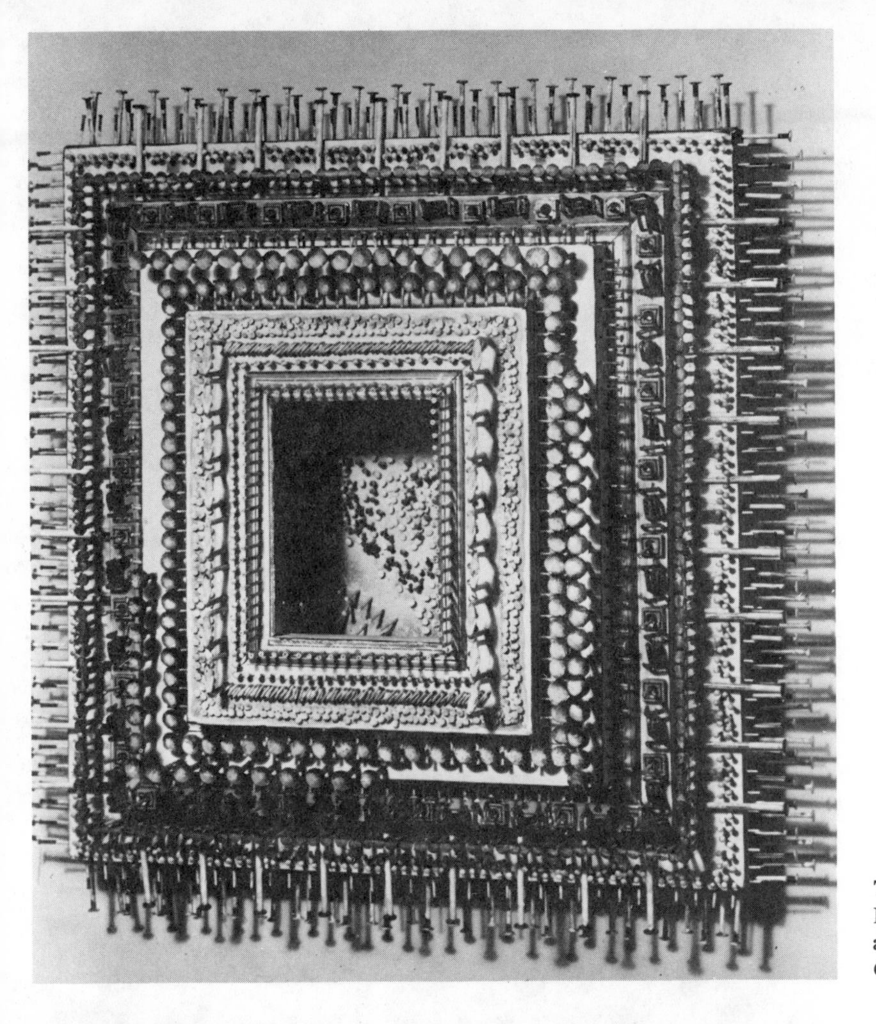

The Jewel. Harriet FeBland. 1967. Frames within frames, with objects added for various textural effects. Courtesy, artist

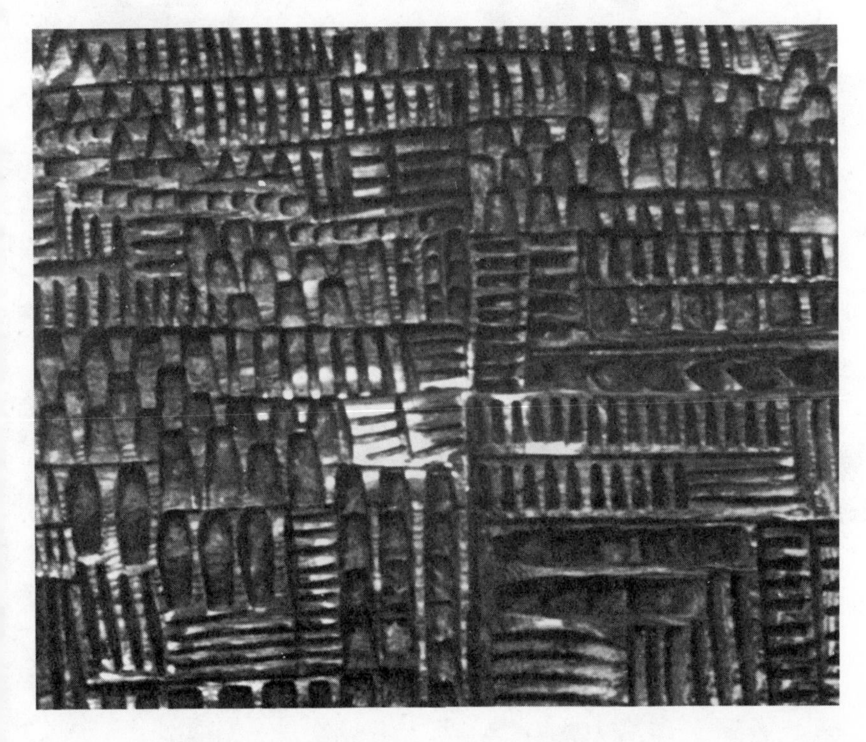

Planet I. (Detail) Robert Pierron. The textural pattern was created by differing shapes, lengths, and repeats of the impression in the wooden surface made with heated screwdriver blades.

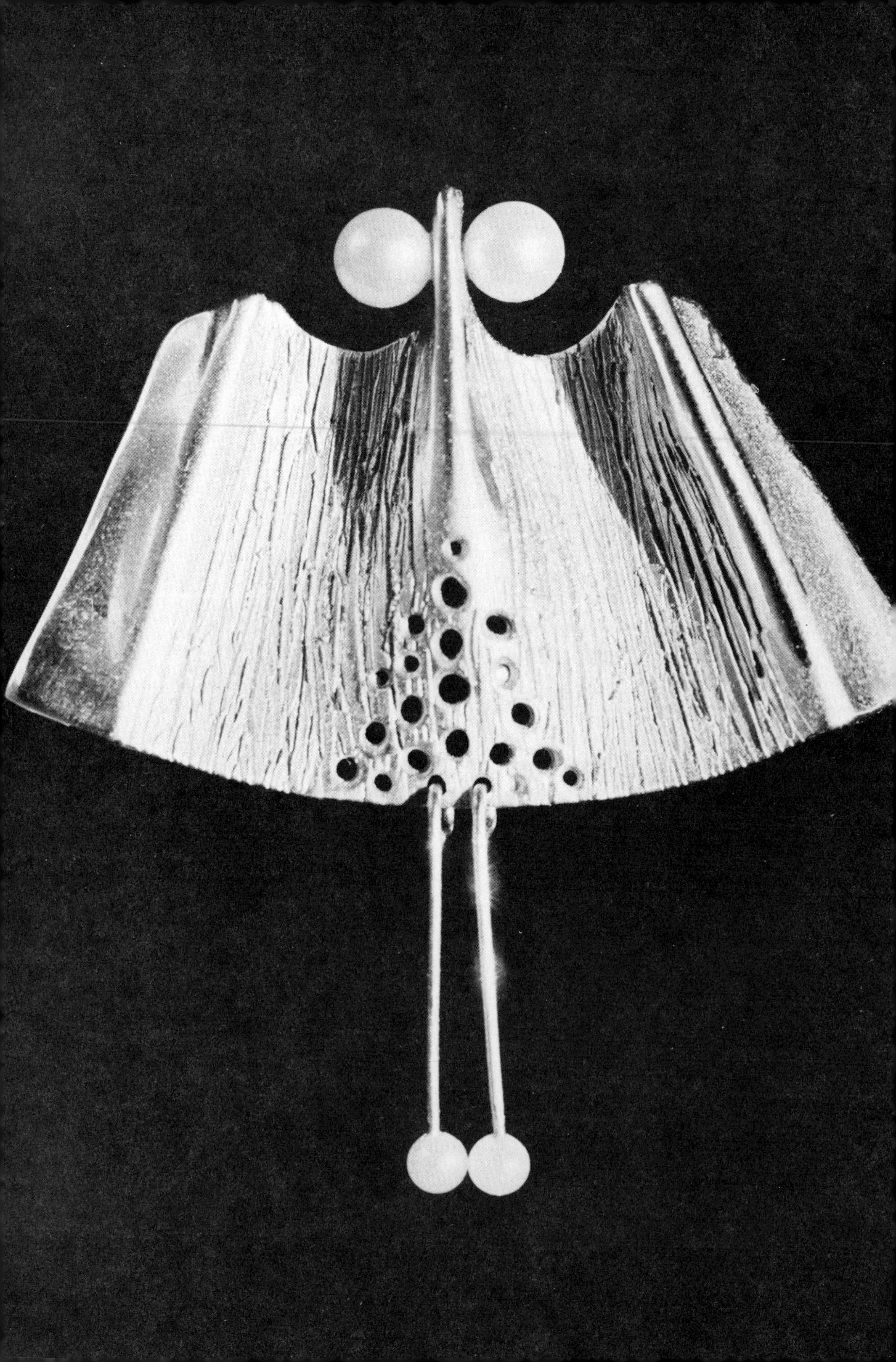

Jewelry. (Opposite) Bob Christiaansen. Cast-gold pin with cultured pearls. The linear striation contrasts with the smooth texture of the pearls.

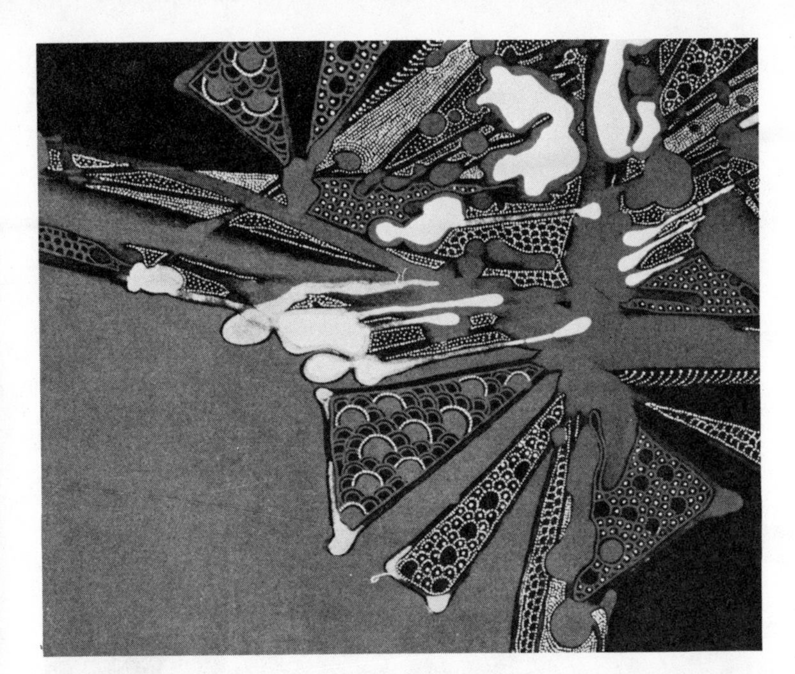

Explosion. Kuwat and Soemihardjo. Contemporary Javanese batik. Courtesy, First Editions, San Jose, California

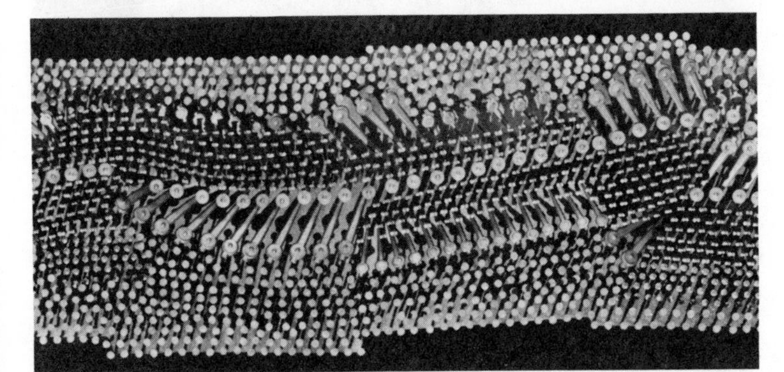

Vertebrate Configuration. David Partridge. 1963. Nails in wood. Photo, Courtesy Tate Gallery, London, S.W.I.

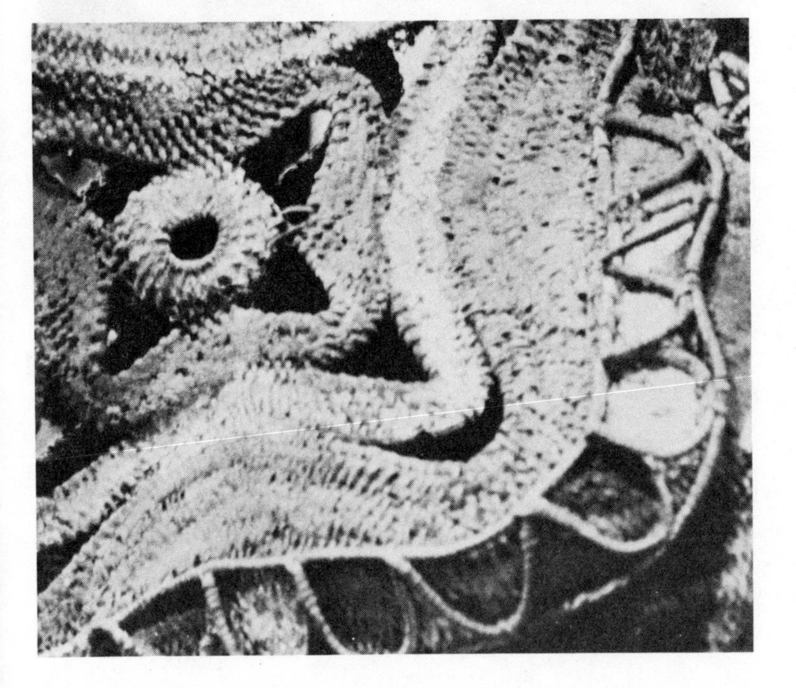

Yam Mask. (Detail) Gawanga–New Guinea. Basketry. The texture results from the weaving, coiling, and materials used.

Texture Study. Claudia Ronaldson. School of The Art Institute of Chicago. Pencil drawing.

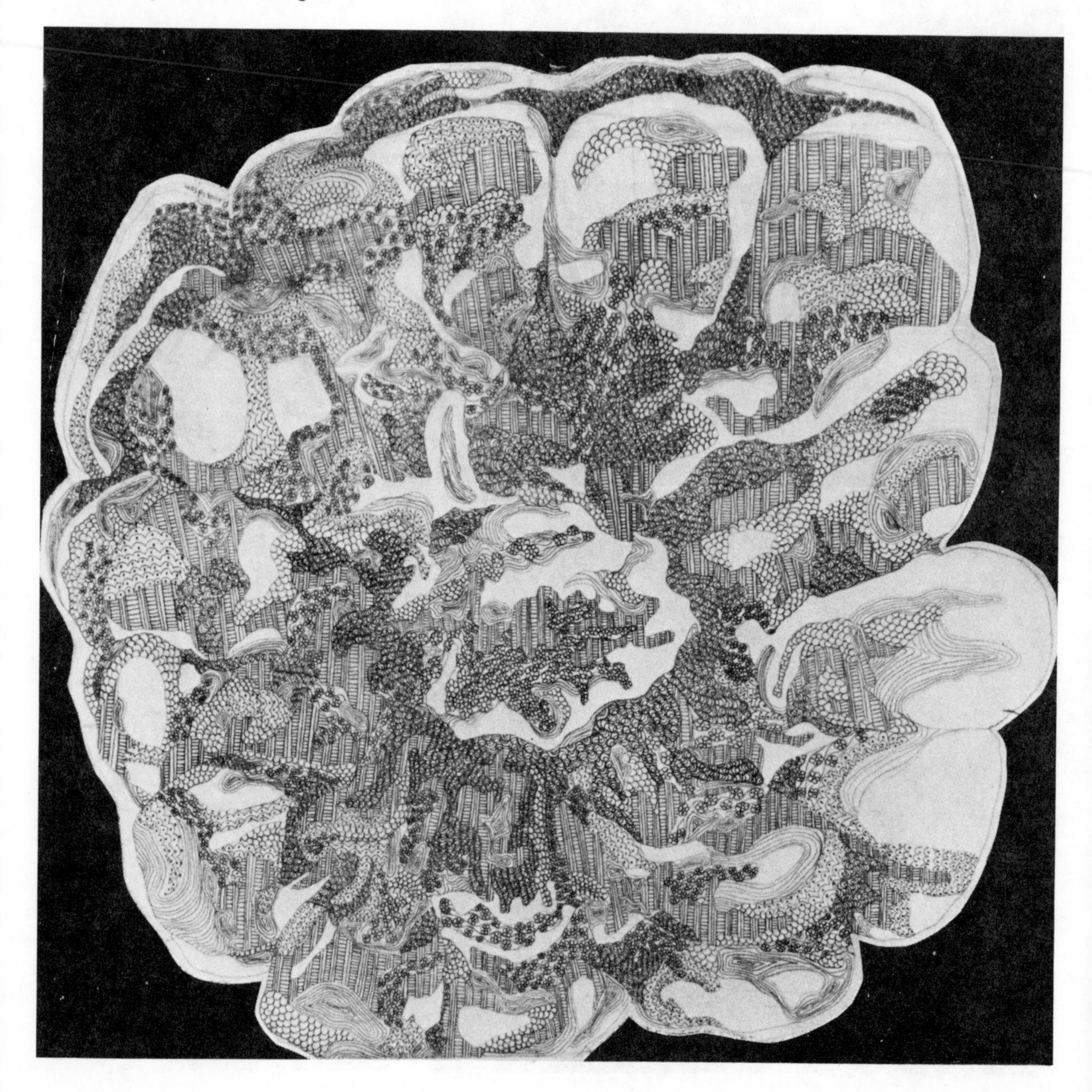

EXERCISES

1 Make rubbings of six *different* textured surfaces with the side of a graphite stick. Position a sheet of paper over the textured surface and hold it in place with one hand. With the other, carefully rub the entire area with the graphite stick.
2 Make rubbings that will result in six different textures of the *same* item. Make the rubbings by stroking a soft lead pencil in one direction across the textural surface. Examples of textured items: manhole covers, weathered wood siding, pavement (sidewalk or street), screening, grillwork, sandpaper.
3 Collect six examples of visual textures from magazines in a limited color range (white, tan, black, brown, plus one brilliant color). These examples could include pictures of flooring planks, letters, and carpeting.
4 Collect six tactile texture collage materials in the same limited color range as above. Some suggested materials might include burlap, sandpaper, emery cloth (black), string, rope, carpet scraps, wood veneer, toothpicks, and velvet. It might be interesting to incorporate the extremes in contrast, such as burlap and velvet, in either contrasting values such as tan and black or in the same value (both tan or black).
5 Design a collage using both the visual and the tactile texture materials collected. Values, shapes, and textures should balance within the composition.

CHAPTER 9

Value

Value may be defined as relative lightness or darkness; the corresponding quality in light is brightness. Value is actually the amount of light a surface reflects. At one extremity of the value scale is white; at the other, black. All the other achromatic (neutral) tones occur between these two extremes. The chromatic (hue) tones also fall between these poles. Every color has the same range from the darkest to the lightest, with a mid-tone created by an equal mixture of black and white (middle-value gray).

Consider a gray scale composed of a range of nine values, starting with WHITE at one end and ending with BLACK at the other:

W = White		HL = High Light	
B = Black		LL = Low Light	
MVG = Middle Value Gray		HD = High Dark	
L = Light		LD = Low Dark	
D = Dark			

By mixing equal portions of:

W+B=MVG
MVG+W=L
MVG+B=D
L+W=HL
L+MVG=LL
MVG+D=HD
D+B=LD

Adding white raises the value.

Adding black lowers the value.

Adding gray (both black and white) raises or lowers the value, depending upon the quantity of each.

Adding a hue pigment of different value also raises or lowers the value. The value of a chromatic pigment cannot be changed without also changing other tonal qualities.

Blackout. Jack Youngerman. Cartoon study for a Gloria F. Ross/Jack Youngerman woven tapestry. 1970. Courtesy, Richard Feigen Gallery, New York

Clothespin. Sarah Hoenecke, student. Hinsdale Central High School, Hinsdale, Illinois. The problem was to relate shapes and balance the values within the format. Photo, Jay Hinz

When the value is affected the intensity will also be affected. The altered tone will be lighter or darker and more neutral than the original and the color will also be altered. Black and white pigment each have a cooling effect on colors when added to them.

When you select value schemes or color schemes for a design, a high-value scheme is one restricted to the upper third of the scale from High Light to Low Light. The intermediate-value scheme is restricted to the middle third of the value scale from Low Light to High Dark or Dark. A low-value scheme includes the lower third of the scale from High Dark to Black. The result would be subtle, muted and somber.

For less subtlety and increased contrast, the scale can be broken into one-half or two-thirds divisions. For maximum contrast, the whole scale from white to black should be used with greater jumps between values.

It is necessary for the designer to understand the value equivalent of hues. The control of contrast is the control of impact.

Gradations of value may be accomplished in a variety of ways. Linear or dotted textures can provide the entire range of grays. The denser the textures (the larger number of dots or lines in a space and the closer these are grouped), the darker the value. The reverse is also true—the wider spaced the textures, the lighter the value. The grays, whether created by painted pigment or by textural density, provide a subtle transition from white to black. This range of contrast is the means used to imitate a graduated light source on a two-dimensional surface and to create the illusion of volume. This control of light and dark forms, called "chiaroscuro," was practiced by sixteenth- and seventeenth-century Mannerist and Renaissance painters, most notably the Dutch.

A number of variations can be accomplished by transposing value arrangements within one design and altering the values of each singular shape in as many ways as possible. Begin by reversing the gray and black areas but leaving the white areas the same. Next, alter several of the flat, gray-value patterns, but use only lines to achieve the same

Value Problem. Judy Truedson, student. Hinsdale Central High School, Hinsdale, Illinois.
Three identical patterns with negative and positive shapes were cut from vertically and horizontally folded strips of black and gray paper. The edge shapes of the gray pattern were to retain the character of, but not duplicate, those of the black pattern. The student split one unit down the center and reassembled it, thereby altering the negative edge pattern.
Photo, Jay Hinz

The Glass Blower. Misch Kohn. 1050–1. Wood engraving. The three major values are represented—black, white, and gray. The gray areas are a result of various densities of different visual textures. Courtesy, The Art Institute of Chicago

Sonata Variation ⋇9. Zbigniew Blazeje. 1965. 24″ high, 24″ wide, 5″ deep. Fluorescent acrylic and phosphorescent paint. Value patterns are created by the applied colors and light and shadow on the three-dimensional geometric forms. Courtesy, Art Gallery of Ontario, Canada

Collage Poster. Leonard Brooks. Different colored brown, black, and cream papers, photographed in black and white, illustrate the dispersement of value in a composition. Courtesy, artist

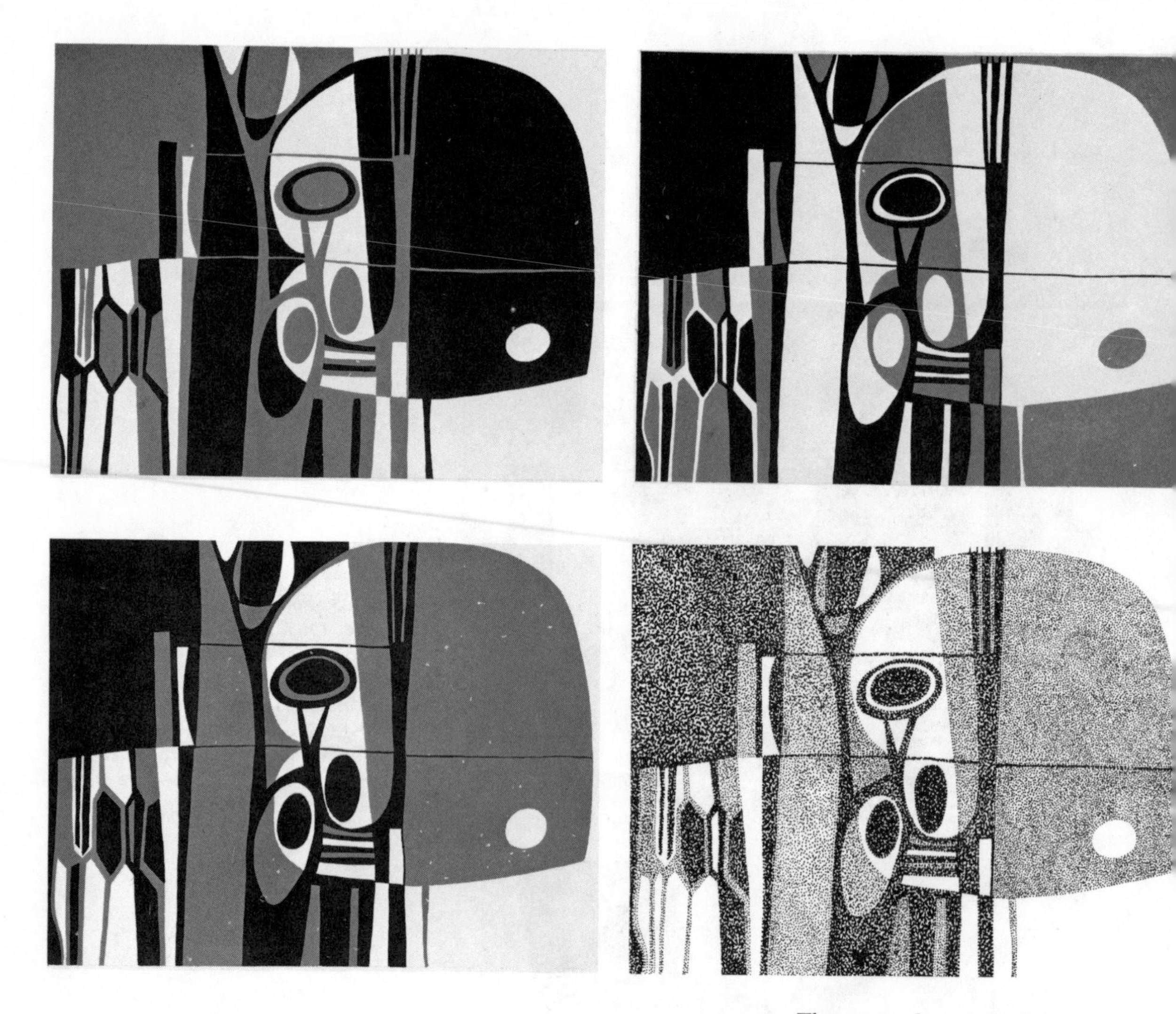

The same value relationships are interpreted in dot using ink. Ink drawings.

Value Transpositions. Bill Hinz. The same composition has different appearances when the values are transposed, and the exercise is excellent for experimenting with designs. These renderings are in Designers' Gouache.

values. Remember, the spacing between the lines will accomplish the value changes. Try the same pattern using only dots.

In geometric black-and-white patterns it is possible to create equal foreground/background shapes, thus making it difficult for the viewer to determine which is which. Two different viewers may see the opposite as figure and background. To produce good design, it is necessary to become as aware of one as you are of the other. The background, or ground, is considered to be the negative space surrounding the positive shapes of the foreground or figure. The figure occupies space. The negative space is empty air space which surrounds form.

The same value relationships are interpreted in line using ink. All drawings by Bill Hinz.

One excellent method for designing is with construction paper representing the three major values: white, black, and gray. Cut simple shapes that are easy to maneuver. By changing their positions you can develop an awareness of ground and its changing relationship to positive shapes. Proportion, relative positioning of shapes and values, and the necessity for the emphasis on size and position become more obvious.

Another method involves beginning with a clothespin, or other simple object, and abstracting it in several stages until it is completely unrecognizable but results in shapes that work together within a common grid.

Bill Hinz. Double-fold symmetrical paper cut design. Positive photostat.

Bill Hinz. Double-fold symmetrical paper cut design. Negative photostat.

Jay Hinz. (Opposite) Double-fold symmetrical paper cut design. Half-negative, half-positive. Photostatic reproduction.

Negative/Positive Values

Symmetrical patterns cut from a folded strip of paper can emphasize negative and positive shapes. If the paper is folded in half twice, a four-way symmetry will result. It might prove interesting to cut two patterns identically alike. Glue one on opposite-value paper. (White on black or black on white.) With the second pattern, cut it apart and rearrange it so as to create an asymmetrical pattern. The design will be harmonious because of the "like" elements it will have in common. This arrangement should prove more challenging than the first.

For additional study and further analyses, make several copies of the same design, cut them apart and reassemble in different ways to yield a variety of units that might be used separately or combined in one complex composition. There are innumerable possibilities for enlargement on this type of experimentation.

Opposite:
Photostat of dot drawing (on page 42). Bill Hinz. Sometimes viewing the same design from a different side can create another feeling or inspire a new design. Try turning any drawing sideways or upside down and extracting another idea from it.

Integration No. 2. Jo Rebert. 22″ high, 30″ wide. Black cutout pasted on white paper. Asymmetrical arrangement of negative and positive lines enclose and imply shape. Courtesy, artist

Rock Garden. Mary Gehr. 1961. Block print.

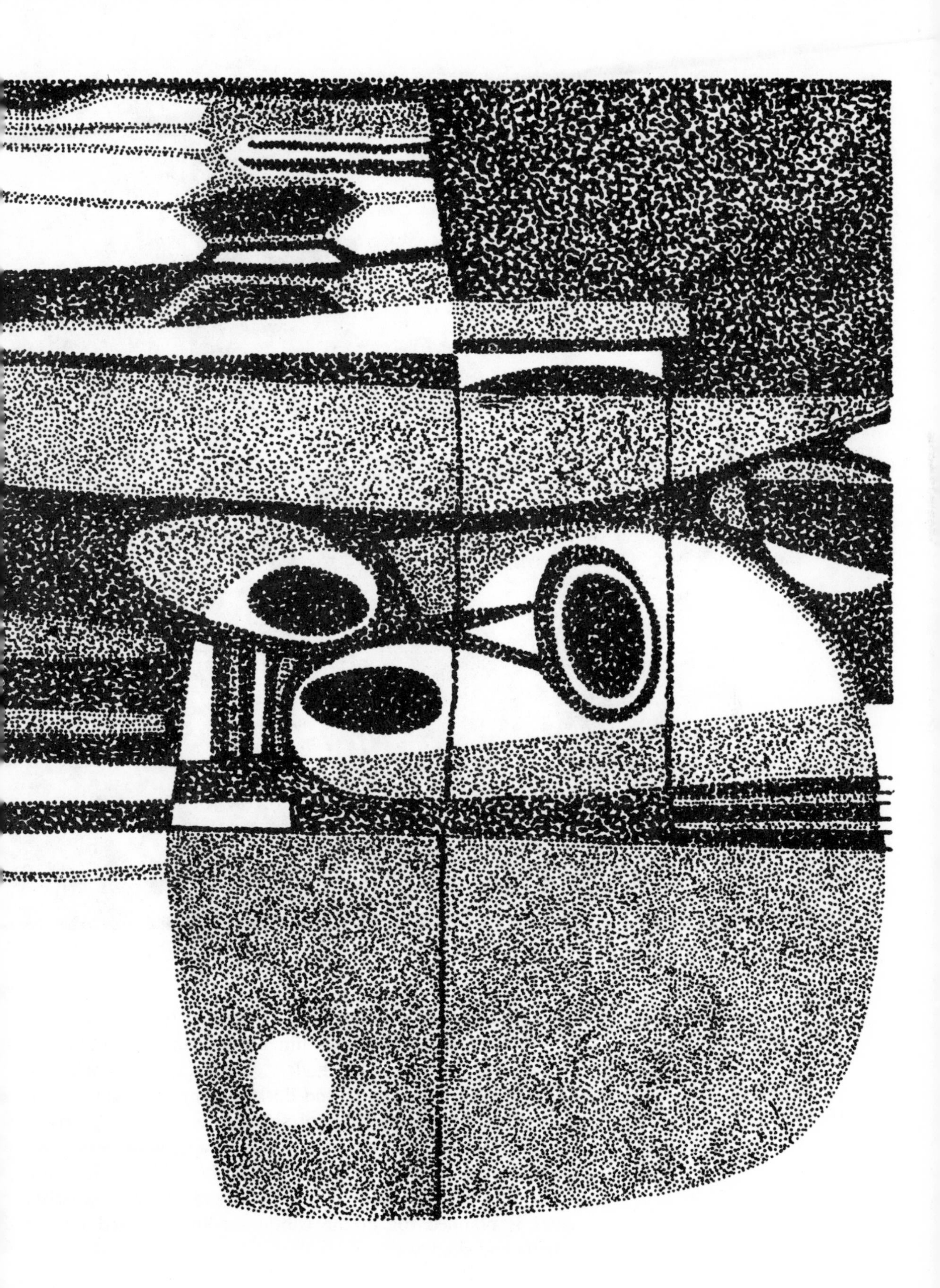

Wood Sculpture. Negative and positive space is carefully designed in a three-dimensional composition. Sizes and shapes are angled differently and vary. Photo, Mel Meilach

The previous examples emphasized value in tonal relationships as it affects two-dimensional surfaces. Value, as it appears in light and shadow, also plays an important role in sculpture. Lights and darks emphasize form. Value is created by the interplay of shadows among the protruding forms and the recessed areas. Negative spaces play against the positive. This is especially evident when the sculpture or relief is of white plaster. Great interest exists and is planned for in the subtle shadows created by the lights and shadows.

EXERCISES

1. Divide a rectangular format into seven balanced black, white, and gray spaces. In seven stages, successively abstract a simple tool or utensil from its recognizable silhouette to its simplest geometric components. The values used for the tool shapes should also balance within the entire composition.
2. Fold a piece of black construction paper vertically. Cut away portions of it so that when it is placed on a white background, equal patterns of black and white will be apparent. The foreground and background should be ambiguous.
3. Use three curvilinear lines to break up a 6″×8″ rectangle. Either end of each line should touch either an edge of the rectangular format or another line. Balance the spaces between the lines with black, white, and gray values. If necessary, to achieve balance, overlap some lines to create a sufficient number of shapes.
4. Transpose the black and white spaces so that what is black in the original design becomes white. The gray areas will remain the same.
5. Make as many other transpositions of this design as you can.
6. Make a low-value scheme of the above design using:
   - A. Vertical lines
   - B. Diagonal lines
   - C. Cross-hatched lines
   - D. Dots
   - E. Any unusual texture of your choice.

CHAPTER 10

Color

Color is the most complex element of design and the most controversial. Many diverse theories exist on the subject, each valid on its own terms. A knowledge of these scientific studies will enable you to comprehend color phenomena so that you can apply the theories and expand them into your own areas of experimentation. This empirical knowledge will aid in developing methods suited to your individual requirements. Rather than present a single approach to color, it is preferable to introduce you to several better-known concepts. The choice is yours. Experimentation and observation are prerequisites for understanding and applying any color theory.

Color is pigment. Color is light. Color is at once a scientific element and an element of design. Scientifically, a color is a ray of light perceived by optical phenomenon. A ray of light consists of different wavelengths and degrees of vibration. When a beam of light passes through a prism, it breaks up into its parts and produces the spectrum. When light hits a surface, it may reflect all colors equally and the eye registers a white; or it could absorb all the waves except one color, which it reflects. Both the nature of color and sight are involved in working with, and understanding, color.

The scientific nature of color is based on physics and psychology; the artistic, or aesthetic, approach to color is based on light, and you should be aware of both aspects.

The experimentation of Sir Isaac Newton in 1667 with varying wavelengths and bending light through a prism resulted in the knowledge of all the colors of the spectrum. The physicist deals with the phenomena of light—the isolation and identification of color through the study of the

Color. Jay Hinz. Cut paper design in different values of white, gray, and black to break up space using the letters from the word "color."

frequencies and wavelengths of rays of light. Physicists further discovered the eye-blends and responses to color. Try looking at the color red for a few minutes. Then look away to a white surface. You will see green. This complement contains all the light rays that red absorbs. This is known as "successive contrast."

The physiologist is concerned with our visual and neurological reaction and response to light and color. The psychologist is interested in our mental reaction and response—the moods and sensations evoked through present to past association with various colors. The historian can trace the course of history and cultures through the selective use of color through the ages. Artists are interested in making color "work" for them. They wish to control it so that it will help them to communicate their desired message or effect.

The pigments used in paint and dyes have many origins, and the source from which they are derived affect their values. Pigment gleaned from organic material such as shell or vegetable will differ from those made synthetically, such as acrylics. Color in light is also important to the artist who uses transparencies to his advantage. When using pigments, combined complementary colors produce gray. When using light, combined complementary colors result in the effect of white light.

Color variations are limitless in variation because the hues may appear differently when translucent, transparent, opaque, shiny, or matte. Actually, the spectrum is vast, but the human brain programs a limited number of strong sensations, thus eliminating the myriad gradations of color that exist in the spectrum.

Chromatic colors are the hues. Achromatic colors are white, gray, and black. White and black are frequently tinted chromatically, giving them "yellowness," "blueness," or "redness." Gray is obtained not only by the mixture of black and white but more richly by the mixture of two complements.

Primary-wheel Theory

All color-pigment-harmony systems differ from one another. The three-color primary-wheel theory is the simplest to understand and a basis for understanding all others. It consists of three primary colors (yellow, blue, and red) which are pure and cannot be mixed. In between each set of primaries, with equal portions of each primary color mixed together, is a secondary color (green, violet, and orange). Tertiary colors are a result of an equal mixture of one primary with one secondary color (yellow+green=yellow-green; green+blue=blue-green; blue+violet=blue-violet; violet+red=red-violet; red+orange=red-orange; orange+yellow=yellow-orange).

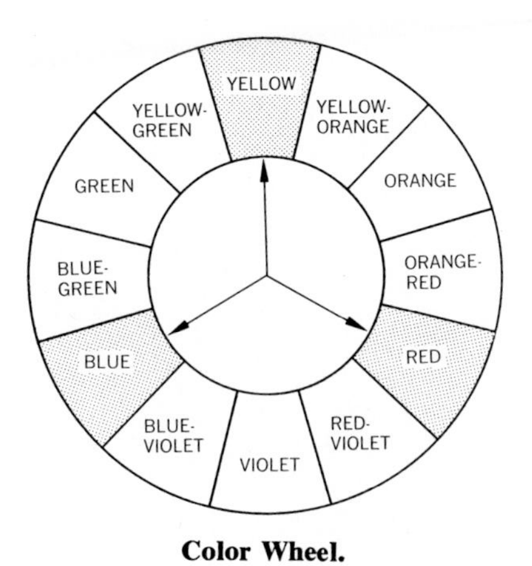

Color Wheel.

The Ostwald Theory

In the Ostwald color theory, the completed circle contains twenty-four hues, with the primaries red, yellow, sea green, and blue, and their secondaries orange, turquoise, leaf green, and purple as a basis. According to this theory, any color may vary in: (1) hue, (2) white content, (3) black content, and (4) black-and-white content. The Ostwald monochromatic triangle consists of varying degrees of color, black, and white. The vertical "leg" of the equilateral triangle consists of white at the top and black at the bottom, with modulated steps of gray in between. The first relationship between the chromatic and achromatic colors is in the "leg" of the triangle that extends from the full-intensity color to white. This is called "the Light Clear Series." The same modulated steps exist between these two extremities, with a gradual progression from the full color toward white. The third "leg" of the triangle consists of the full-intensity color at one end and black at the other. This is known as "the Dark Clear Series." The same orderly progression of steps occurs between the full color and black. The last modification involves the completion of the inner triangle with modular steps of the full color mixed with black and white to produce the grayed colors.

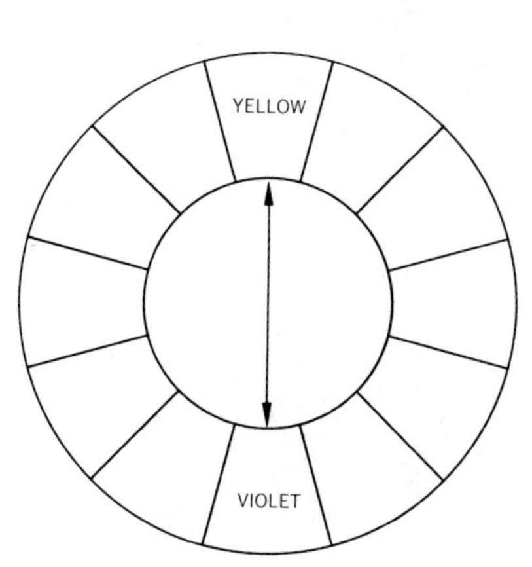

Complementary colors are directly opposite each other.

The Munsell Theory

Munsell theorized red, yellow, green, blue, and purple to represent the five primary colors. The Munsell Color Solid shows the light colors at a level near white, the dark colors at a level near black. The high-intensity colors extend farther from the gray scale than do the paler colors.

In all theories, color has three qualities: hue, value, and intensity. Hue is that quality which distinguishes one color from another. The value, or dark and light, is referred to as tone. Tones are grayed hues achieved by mixing the pure color with black and white, or the complement to it. Chromatic colors have the quality of hue in them; the achromatic colors remain neutral. The chroma or intensity in the Munsell system refers to the quality of saturation to the fullest degree of the color content.

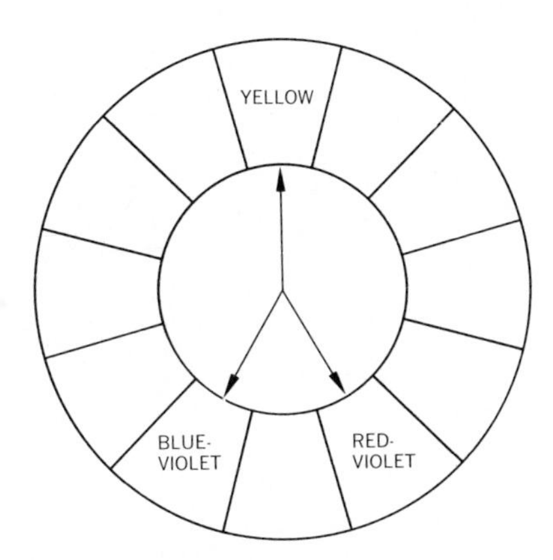

Near-complementary colors lie nearly opposite one another.

The thermal properties of color include warmth and coolness. The colors on the red-yellow portion of the wheel are considered warm; those on the blue-green portion are re-

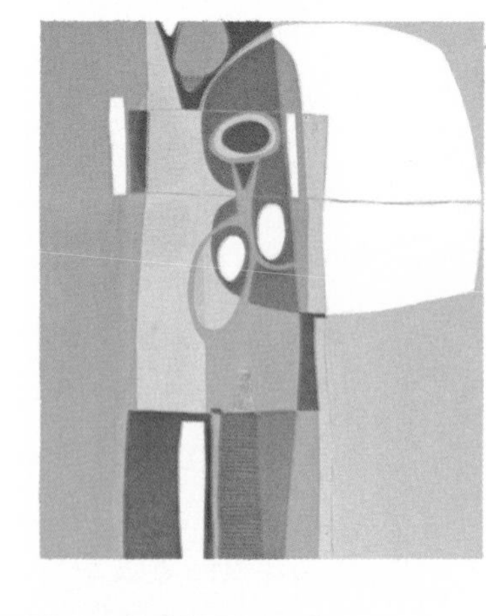

Hooked Wall Hanging. Bill Hinz. Persian wool. There is a balance of values in the curvilinear space divisions. The dominant green and red portions each have some yellow in them for unity.

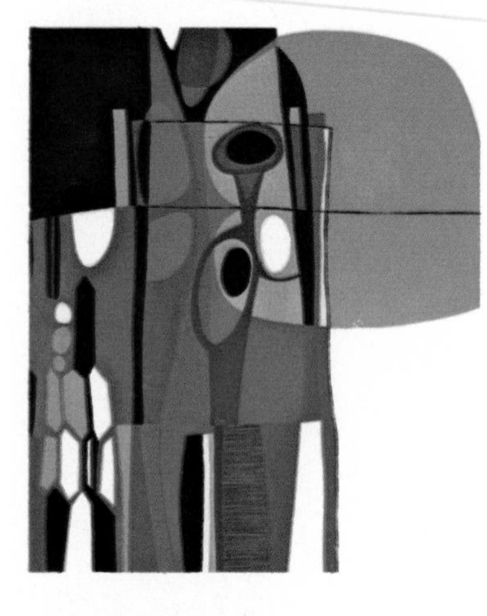

Rendering. Bill Hinz. Designer's Gouache. Three different color schemes applied to the same design give it three distinct appearances. The space is broken up asymmetrically.

Rendering. Bill Hinz. Designer's Gouache. Design for a circle utilizes curved linear segments and a close color harmony.

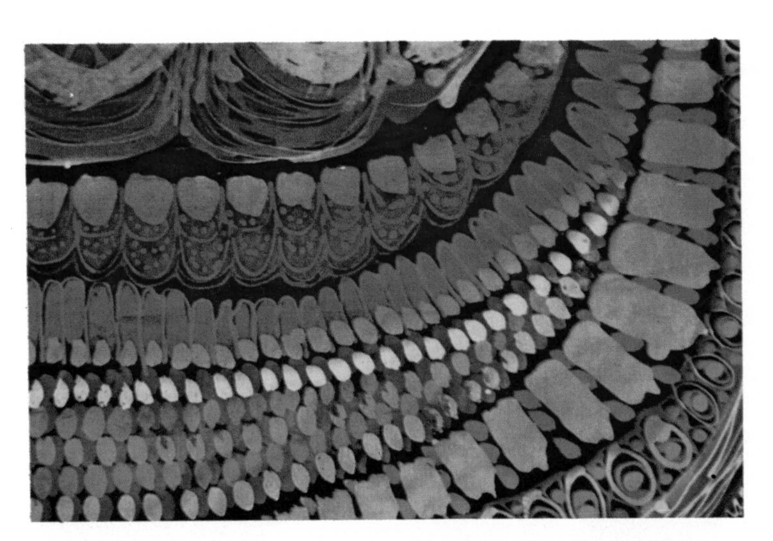

Chrysalis. (Detail) Bernice Colman. Batik. The color division has cool blue separated from warm red and orange tones by a transitional red violet which has both blue and red in it. Courtesy, artist

Vase. Bob Christiaansen. Bronze chased and repousséd. The reflective surface of the undulating forms picks up colors from the environment.

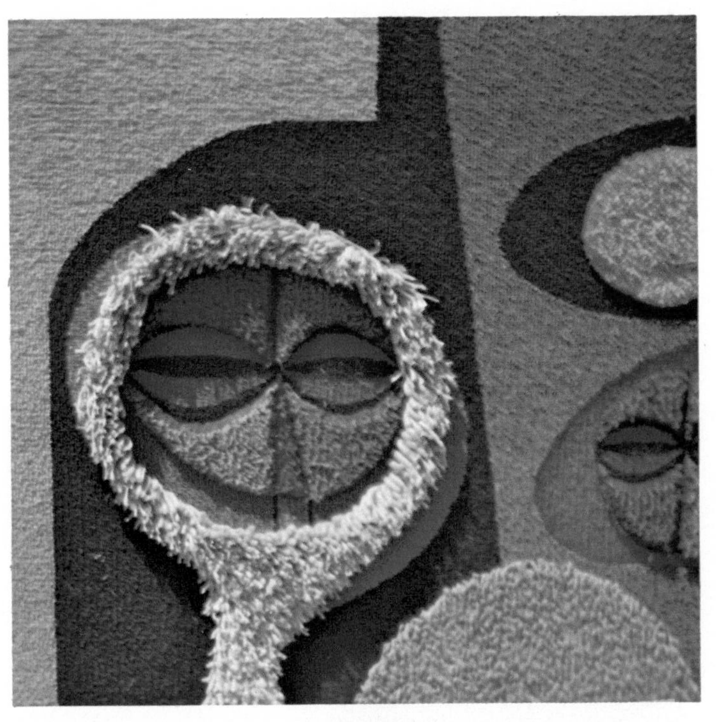

Golf Pros. (Detail) Bill Hinz. Hooked rug. Colors are accented by the supportive use of black. The yarns protrude from the backing in varying heights, textures, and colors. Collection, Dr. and Mrs. M. Meilach, Chicago

Weaving. Lois Constantine. Wool with metal. The dynamic shapes within the design are complemented by the intensity of the colors.

Peeling Paint. Dona Meilach. Photo. The eye of the photographer has selected a close-up detail of a weathered circus wagon for its beauty of texture and color.

Solar. Elenhank Designers, Inc. A mural print for drapery or wallcovering. The fold-dye technique was the source for the design and resulted in the color repetition. Courtesy, artist

The Blanchet Doors. Mabel Hutchinson. Different exotic woods provide natural color for the pair of doors that are carefully balanced for design and color. Courtesy, artist

ferred to as cool. This, also, is relative. A green with more blue in it will be cooler than one with more yellow in it. Warm colors advance; cool colors recede.

Color Schemes

There are various color-scheme possibilities.

The analogous arrangement uses colors that are adjacent or next to one another in sequence on the color wheel (e.g., red, red-orange, orange, yellow-orange, yellow, etc.).

Another scheme is based on *complementary colors*—those that are directly across from each other on the color wheel. If a line were drawn from yellow through the center of the circle to the opposite side, the complement would be violet. A split complement would be one color plus the color on either side of its complement (yellow, red-violet, blue-violet).

A *monochromatic color scheme* involves one color plus its tints and shades. A tint is a color to which white or extender has been added. A shade is a color to which black has been added. Therefore, a monochromatic color scheme might be light blues, middle blues, dark blues. "Mono" means one; "chroma" means color.

The *triad color scheme* is based on an equilateral triangular arrangement on the color wheel. Each color is equidistant from the other two comprising the triangle. The primary and secondary colors are triadic in arrangement on the wheel. Another example would be red-orange, yellow-green, and blue-violet.

Color is changed by an alteration in its contrast. This is the "energy" of color. This causes color to vibrate. Color will create the illusion of expansion or contraction dependent upon the relationship of it to its background. This "energy" is dependent upon a second color and our perception of the interaction of the two.

"Successive contrast" was mentioned previously. Another phenomenon similar in nature is seen by placing a medium gray square on green and a similar square on red. In each case, the gray appears to be tinged with the complementary of the color upon which it is placed. This is called "simultaneous contrast."

A design made up only of analogous colors will produce a peaceful, harmonious effect. Perhaps it may seem too monotonous (depending upon the intention of the artist). In this case, a contrasting complementary color may give it the "punch" that is necessary. Designs composed only of complementaries may need some analogous colors to "quiet" them down.

Josef Albers is a contemporary artist with an approach to color that suggests there are no absolute qualities in color, and that color does not remain constant. Color is relative to that which surrounds it. The same color in a different environment will appear differently. Albers, as well as other current artists, are more interested in color dynamics than in traditional color-mixing theories. He encourages his students to learn the many properties of color and their inexhaustible combinations, emphasizing the interaction and interdependence of colors.

Colors are always seen in combination. Therefore, relationships should always be of concern to the designer. Yellow will appear differently when seen in combination with black than it will when combined with green or with red. The yellow will change in hue and value. This is referred to as "color induction." A gray square will change value when its background value is switched from black to white.

It cannot be overemphasized that the best way to learn to use color is to USE it! Experiment! Paint each of several sheets of paper different colors of the color wheel. Also, paint sheets of various lightened, grayed, and darkened hues. Cut some shapes from each sheet of color. Maneuver them about on contrasting sheets. Play! Observe! Learn!

CHAPTER 11

Repeat Pattern

Repetition of shape will produce patterns, either random or regular. A random pattern is based on unmeasured repetition and can be observed in examples throughout this book and in nature itself. Regular pattern is based on repeated units at measured intervals. Such patterns generally follow one of the basic networks: straight cross (with the square or rectangle); brick, or stagger; half-drop; diamond; triangle; ogee; hexagon, or scale. Characteristic of the basic grids, the spaces interlock.

The straight-cross repeat is produced by intersecting vertical and horizontal lines which are perpendicular to each other.

The brick, or stagger, pattern results from horizontal alternation, the half-drop from vertical alternation. The conventional arrangement of both repeats is based on shifting the next row one-half a unit.

Circular motifs diagrammed to fit within either network hide the actual network and appear to be in a diamond.

The true diamond is a perfect square resting vertically on one point.

The triangle is a divided diamond with considerable flexibility. Triangles can be assembled to form squares, rectangles, parallelograms, hexagons, and octagons.

The ogee is derived from the diamond but is based on the S curve. Ogees may be used horizontally or vertically. The shapes dovetail so that the contours of the neighboring shapes will not leave spaces in between. Because of its fluidity of form, the ogee lends itself particularly to curved motifs.

If the radius of a circle is marked off repeatedly on its circumference, six equidistant points result. A line con-

Multiple Image. David Berglund. A view of the John Hancock Building, Chicago. Composed of sixteen individual prints. Courtesy, artist

Eight Repeat Patterns.

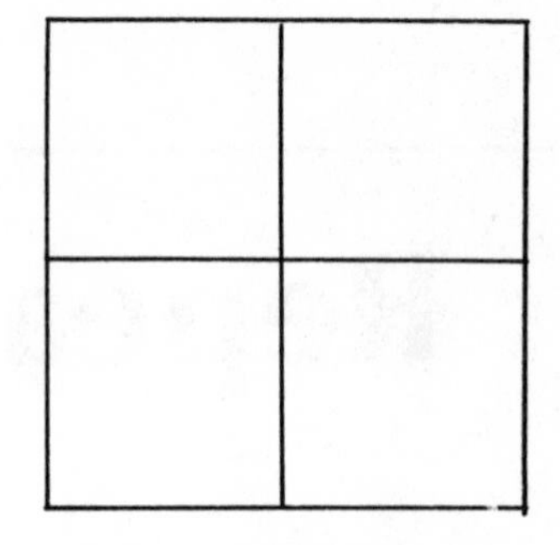

Straight-cross Repeat.

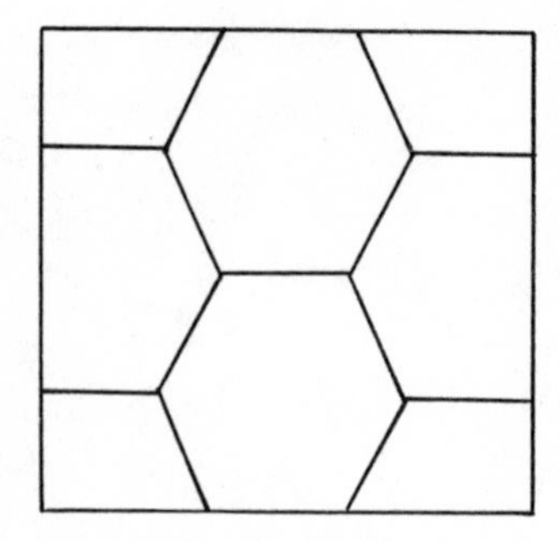

Hexagonal Repeat.

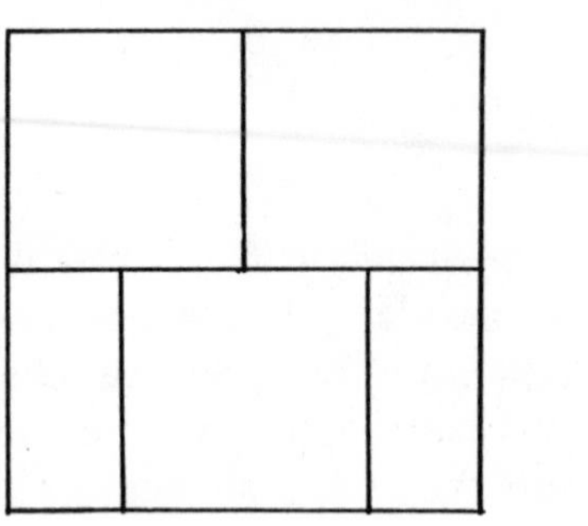

Stagger Repeat.

Scale Repeat.

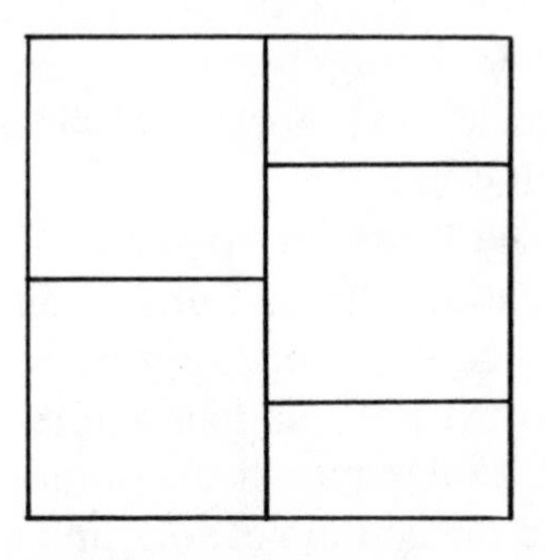

Half-drop Repeat.

Ogee Repeat.

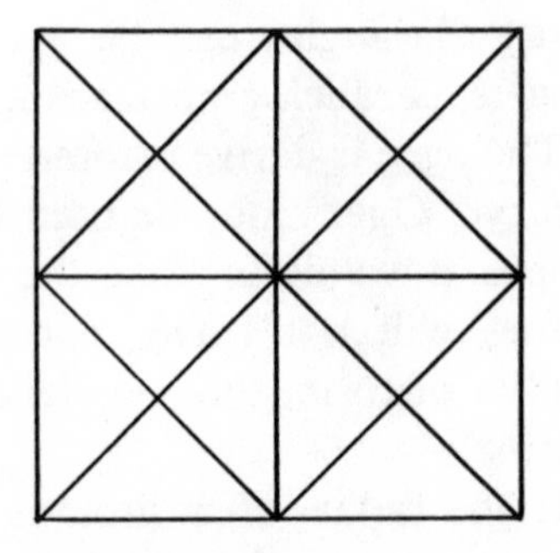

Triangular Repeat.

Diamond Repeat.

Jacks. (Detail) Tony Monaco. Straight-cross repeat. Silk-screened fabric.

Wrought Iron Door. Louis L. Sullivan. Courtesy, Art Institute of Chicago

Framed Fringe. (Detail) Linda Ulvestad Fischer. Collage. Repeat patterns overlaid and accomplished with a variety of materials such as ovals of fine stovepipe wire woven into heavy copper printing paper and surrounded by printing and drawing papers. A top layer of heavy mat board contains thirty-five rectangular openings, covered with a quarter-inch-thick acrylic sheeting. Courtesy, artist

The Family. (Detail of a Triptych) Jennifer Lew. 1967. Observe especially the repeat of the scale shape in different sizes. Photo, William Eng Collection, Constance Y. Furuta

Yardage No. 2. (Detail) Jennifer Lew. 1967. Wall hanging. 72″ high, 42″ wide. Batik on silk broadcloth using the tjanting tool for dominant linear repeats. Photo, William Eng Collection, Marlyn Hudson

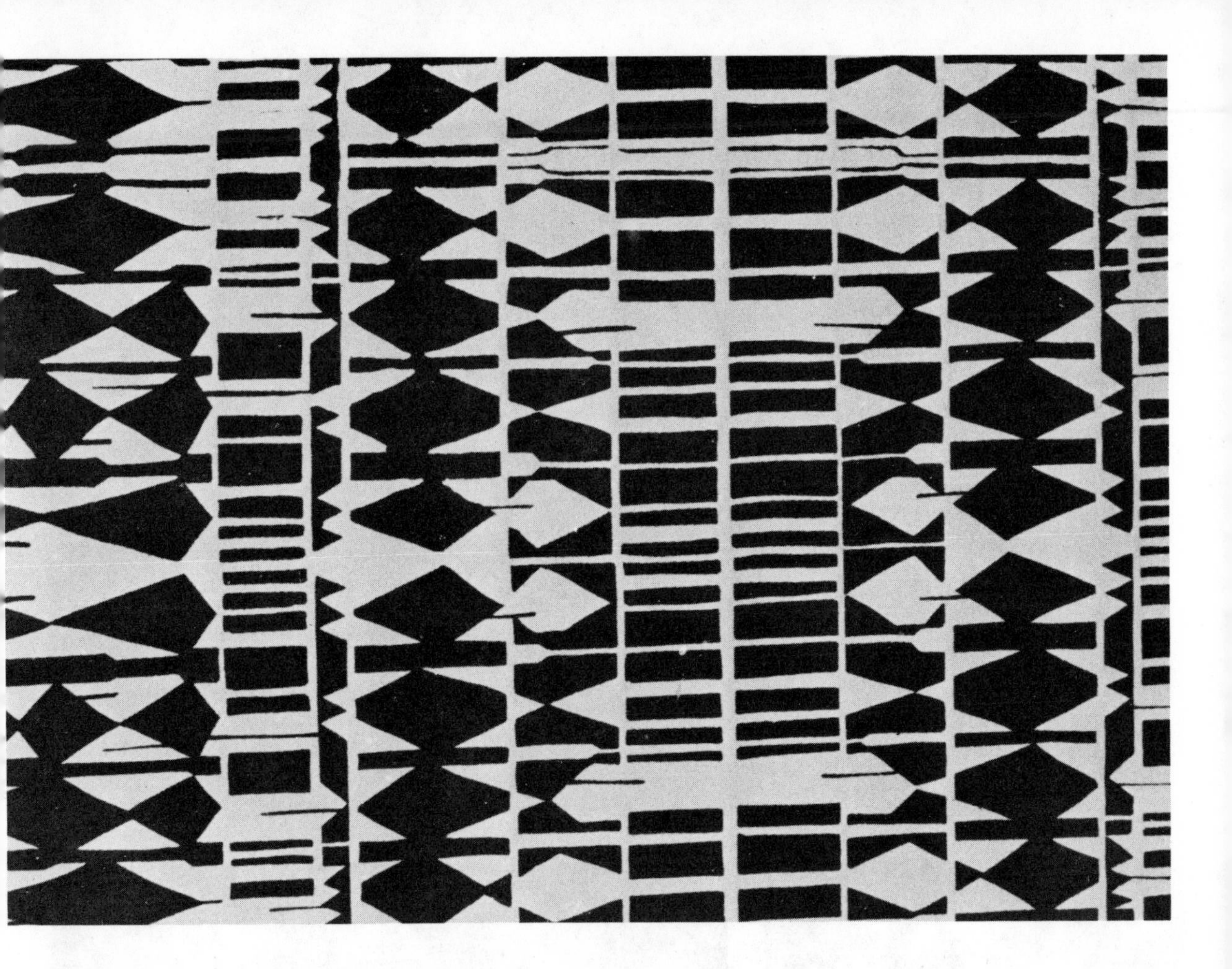

necting these points produces an equilateral hexagon which will repeat itself infinitely without producing any remaining spaces.

Pentagons and octagons also offer versatile compositional units but, when they are repeated, negative spaces are created.

Any grouping of touching circles will effect a pattern with negative spaces between. For this reason, the circle cannot produce a true interlocking network.

Overlapping circles will produce a network of scales. Circles are commonly designed as units and then repeated on other networks, more commonly on the brick, or stagger, or on the half-drop.

To test a repeat pattern, carve the unit into an artgum eraser with a linoleum cutter. Use a ruler and a sharp pencil. Delicately rule out the repeat networks you wish to try, using the dimensions of the carved surface. Press the carved eraser onto an inked stamp pad, then press onto one portion of the ruled grid. Repeat until you have filled in the grids. This method will enable you to quickly see the effects of the various repeats.

Geometric. Tony Monaco. Straight-cross repeat. Silk-screened fabric.

Interrupted Pattern. Ceiling of a railroad station. Photo, Jay Hinz

Matiers. (Right below) Zolton Kemeny. 1958. Aluminum and plastic. Repeat squares within squares in different sizes and values. Courtesy, Hanover Gallery, London, England

Palm Tree Trunk. A repeat pattern in a natural growth.

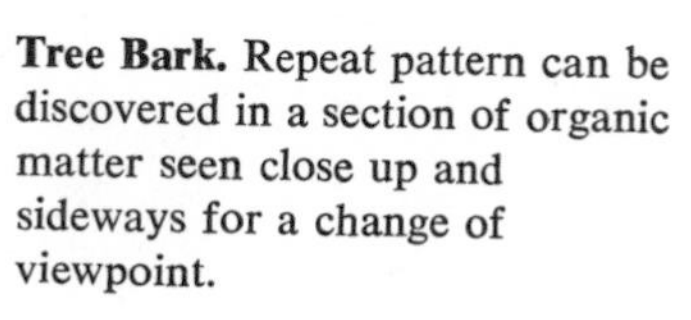

Tree Bark. Repeat pattern can be discovered in a section of organic matter seen close up and sideways for a change of viewpoint.

Onions. A random repeat.

Mattress Springs. Straight-cross repeat in manufactured merchandise. Photo, Mel Meilach

EXERCISES

1 *Straight-cross Repeat.* Break up a 1″ square using only two other squares. These may be concentric or overlapping. Fill in the shapes with black, white, and gray values.
Using the same design, alter the value as many ways as you can; replace some solid shapes with outline.
Make a grid of 1″ squares, eight squares across and eight squares down. Arrange the varied-value patterns in a pleasing repetition within this grid.

2 Cut a 1″ square apart. Trim some off each edge. Reassemble. Place on top of a 1″ square of contrasting value.
   A. Rotate the design to fit four times into a 2″ square.
   B. Rotate and flop over the unit as many ways as you can to create variations in the design.

3 *Half-drop and Stagger Repeats.* Try the same designs as above extended to fit a rectangle in the:
   A. Half-drop Repeat
   B. Stagger Repeat.

4 *Triangular Repeat.* Break up a triangle with other triangles (shapes and lines) using all three values. Repeat in the triangular repeat.

5 *Diamond Repeat.* Create a design within a diamond with straight-edged shapes and lines using all three values. Repeat with:
   A. Identical-value placement
   B. Alternating the value.

6 *Ogee Repeat.* Create a design within an ogee shape, using black, white, and gray shapes and lines. Repeat.

7 *Hexagonal Repeat.* Break up the hexagon with triangles, chevrons, circles, or diamonds in black and white. Repeat with variation of value, or change from shape to line, or use a combination of both.

8 *Circle.* Design a circle within a square. Repeat.

9 *Scale.* Create a design within the scale shape, using curves primarily (either shape or line or both).
Repeat:
   A. In scale repeat
   B. In alternating diagonal rows.

Solar Screen. (Detail) Martin Metal. Steel and copper. Detail of sculpture relief on façade. Courtesy, artist

Geometric Repeat Pattern I. Student exercise. Straight-cross repeat.

Geometric Repeat Pattern II. Student exercise. Straight-cross repeat.

CHAPTER 12

Designing for a Circle

The circle, without beginning and without end, symbolizes eternity. According to Webster, "A circle is a closed plane curve such that all of its points are equidistant from a point within, the center." Many designs within a circle are inspired by natural forms. Some cultural and historical circular designs are based upon mathematical concepts.

Flowers, such as chrysanthemums, or daisies, with patterned arrangements and overlapping petals, provide inexhaustible models for duplicating, simplifying, or elaborating within a circle. The edge of the circle does not necessarily remain a self-contained rim. Petals ending at the rim can produce an irregular edge, yet still imply a circle. The simplicity of the circular shape invites a wide approach to diversifying it.

Other objects that offer symmetrical patterns and spiraling progressions for creative improvisation are monads (single units as an atom), sea shells, snow crystals, stars, starfish, tree sections, and wheels. Such structures conform within the perimeter of a circle and offer beautiful possibilities for linear divisions and designs.

The monad has many symbolic meanings: duality, light and dark, sun and moon, heaven and earth, Yang and Yin, male and female, positive and negative. Snow crystals are formed of two essential shapes: slender, needlelike axial bundles of sharp rods and thin hexagonal flat surfaces. Stars usually are considered to be five-sided, each point resting upon the circumference of the circular figure. The wheel is based upon an axial intradivision of the circle. The number of divisions is arbitrary.

Two considerations should remain foremost when designing for any particular shape: (1) retain the outer shape,

Four Mile Polychrome Bowl.
Homolovi (No. 1) Arizona.
Photo, Field Museum of Natural History, Chicago

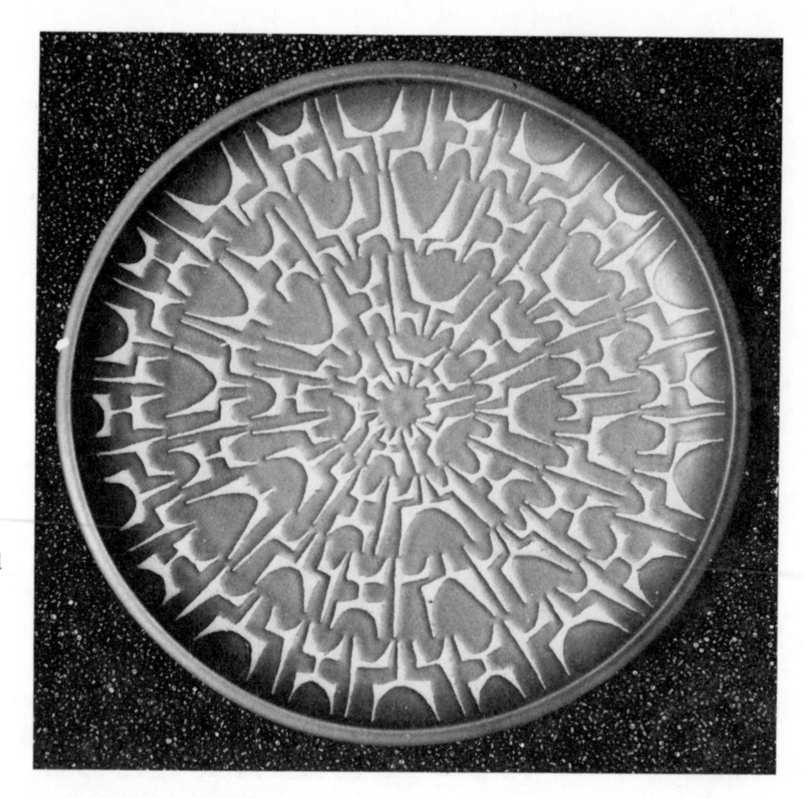

Large Round Plate Form. Clyde Burt. The design within the circle was intended to give almost equal space and interest to the positive and negative areas. Courtesy, artist

even when subdividing its interior with more complex delineations, and (2) retain and exploit the essence of the material from which the design is crafted. For example, water colors should express fluidity, spontaneity, and transparency; they should not be used as poster paints. Continuity of form, intradivisions of that form, compatibility of material to form, and compatibility of technique to material should interweave to become one inseparable, unified "whole."

Frank Lloyd Wright, the noted twentieth-century American architect, professed that structure is an organic unit in which the parts of the interior space flow one into another and by way of the exterior to the surrounding site. He writes, ". . . the ideal of an organic architecture forms the origin and source, the strength and, fundamentally, the significance of everything ever worthy of the name of architecture. By organic architecture I mean an architecture that develops from within outward, in harmony with the conditions of its being as distinguished from one that is applied from without." Mr. Wright's philosophy, still valid today, applies to the designing of all shapes and spaces: two-dimensional, three-dimensional, interior, exterior, negative, or positive.

Spotlights of Las Vegas #2. Jo Rebert. The figures were designed to be viewed from one direction but the calligraphic rhythm permits the circle to be revolved on its axis without losing the interest of the inner lines and forms. Courtesy, artist

To break up or unify the space within a circle for a design, you must preserve the circular form and retain the circumference. It is important to at least suggest the edge to assure the impact of the circular form.

A designed circle can be approached many ways: It can be completely filled as a solid, it can retain only the outer circular rim or portions of it, it can create rings of pattern within the circular shape, or it can be broken into circular symmetrical divisions.

It is possible to retain the circle in its solid form as a unit of design. This simple, solid circular form can be used as a solitary unit or it can be repeated in any of the grid arrangements. (See Chapter 11, "Repeat Pattern.") The circle can be identical in size and value, it can be alternated in value, or altered in size or proportion so that some shapes become variations of the circle, such as an oval. The same examples can be translated into line designs instead of solid forms.

A symmetrical division of space can be either bilateral or radial. Bilateral symmetry assumes each side of a median line or plane corresponds identically to the other side. This is frequently referred to as a "mirror image." Radial symmetry involves more than two divisions of the circular space. This concept of radial symmetry suggests a number of divisions which radiate away from the common center toward all portions of the edge to result in pie shapes. Another type of circular symmetry consists of circular bands spaced away from the common center as concentric rings. Symmetry provides a means of creating interest throughout the entire shape without emphasizing any one area.

To create emphasis, if desired, the symmetry can be altered to achieve asymmetrical arrangements. Use irregular spacings between the shapes, along the rim, or facing from the center of the circle out to the edge. The same shapes could be used, but the intervals of spacing could be increased, or decreased, and the direction, density, or value of the dots, lines, or shapes could be changed.

Shapes compatible to the circle are those with something in common with it. Dots are a minute duplication of the circular motif. In concentrated areas they can amass together to form circles. Separated, they become harmonious building units or textures that will enhance the circular form.

All elements used to create the break up of the circular space should have something in common with the circle. If straight lines or straight-edged shapes are used, there must be some transition between them and the curves of the circle. Perhaps dots at the ends of straight lines or dots connecting or separating linear segments will provide the needed transition. Curved segments combined with straight ones will accomplish the same end. Free-flowing, curvilinear lines will emphasize the fluidity of the shape itself without restricting the inner action to its static uninterrupted symmetry.

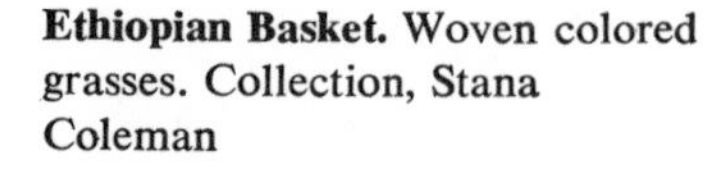

Ethiopian Basket. Woven colored grasses. Collection, Stana Coleman

Primitif. Jennifer Lew. 1967. Wall hanging. Batik on silk shantung. Photo, William Eng Collection, Richard M. Proctor

More complex variations and expansions of the circle and its divisions are numerous. Circular shapes may be altered in gradual sequence, with subtle degrees of change occurring on one segment of the form's edge or on more than one segment of the circular rim. The changes may occur in the center of the form, at its corners, or along its edges.

Fascination with a shape, the material selected to work with, and the manipulation of it can result in a creative fulfillment of a specific space requirement. The technique employed will depend upon the medium selected. Techniques may include either high or low relief. This shallow third dimension utilizes a depth interest through the value contrasts of the light and shadow patterns that result. A relief can be created by carving, or incising, into the surface or by adding materials to the surface to create dimension such as paint impasto, glaze, coils of clay or raffia, and others.

Ceramic objects have traditionally been a unique material for circular interpretation. Pottery of North American Indians, including the Anasazi, Hohokam and Homolovi, and the Classic Mimbres cultures, provides a good source of design inspiration based upon the geometric form. The circular form of an earthenware plate or bowl offers both the outer (convex) and inner (concave) surfaces for design. These can be treated as one continuous design or as two individual patterns. When some continuity between the convex and concave surfaces is planned, the edges of some of the shapes and lines from the pattern on one surface should be extended onto the other surface as well. These extensions will provide the necessary transition be-

Pillow-Salami. Edna Martin. Embroidered linen. Courtesy, The Cooper-Hewitt Museum of Decorative Arts and Design, New York

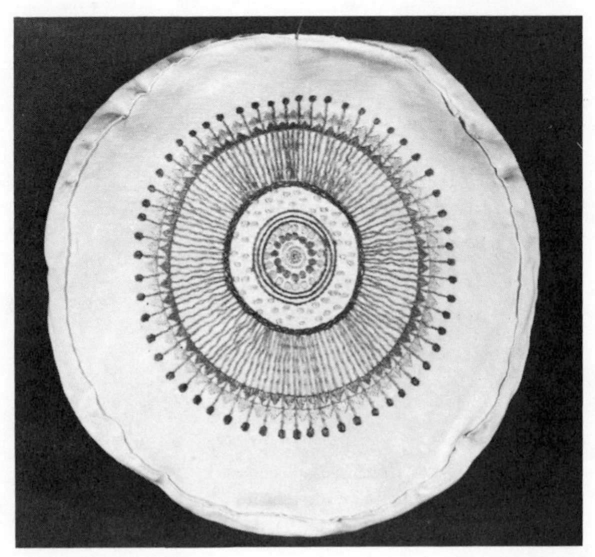

Round Pillow-Dillkrona. Eva Kohlmark. (Sweden) White linen, embroidered in white and shades of green and gray. Pattern is based on an open flower head. Courtesy, The Cooper-Hewitt Museum of Decorative Arts and Design, New York

Necklace. Bob Christiaansen.
Cast with stones and string.

Pin. Bob Christiaansen. Cast and
forged in sterling, with leather
and carnelian stones.

Basket. Dona Meilach.
Figure-eight basket coiling. Fringe cords added. Beige linen over a cotton clothesline core. Extra core rope was added for handles using figure-eight wrapping.

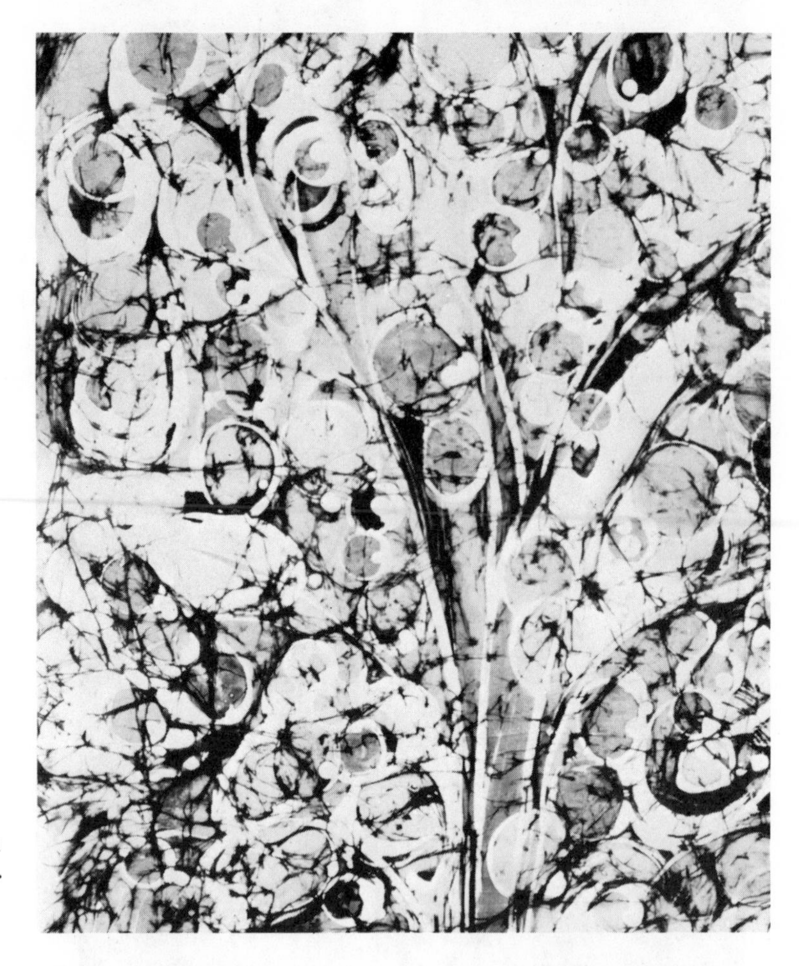

Sugar Plum Tree. (Detail) Blanche Carstenson. Batik. Orange-juice cans dipped in wax created the original resist circles. Colored circles were added in subsequent dye baths.

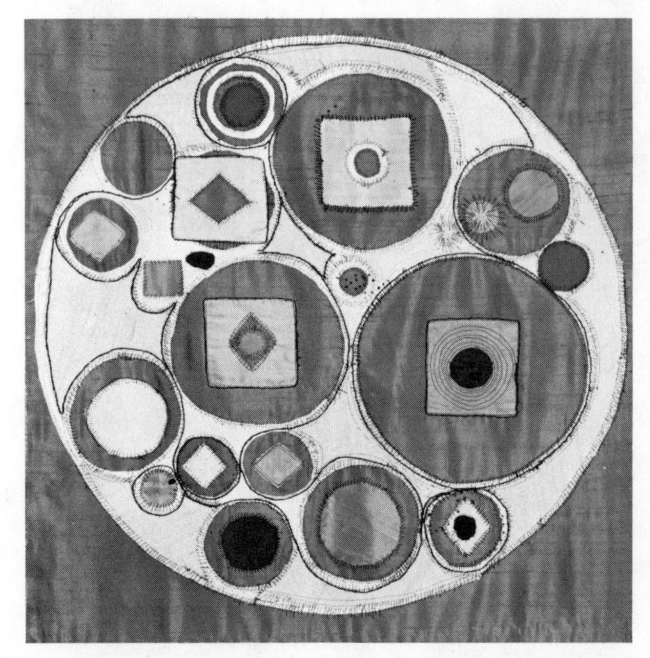

Circles. (Detail) Anna Pickering. 1967. Appliqué using silk fabrics with machine and hand stitching. Photo, "Judge" Industrial Photographers

Birth of a Star. Thea Tewi. Stalactite. 1968. Approximately 20″ diameter. A circle in the third dimension with the use of a circular protrusion and negative shape. Courtesy, artist

Macramé. (Detail) Leora Stewart. Circular ringed negative spaces are incorporated into the knotted hanging. Courtesy, artist

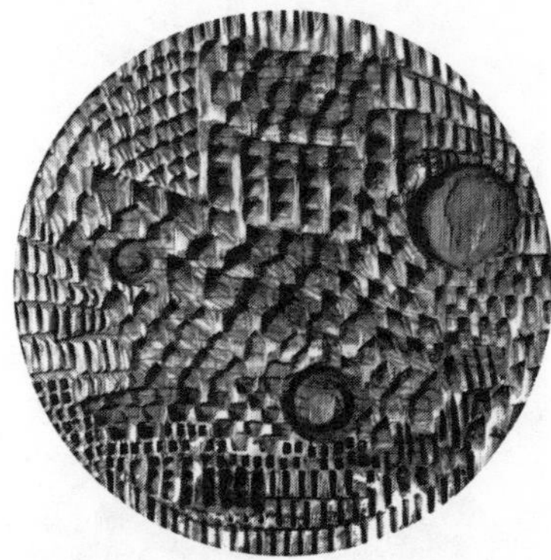

Planet. (Detail) Robert Pierron. The tool marks stop at the edge of the circle, defining the form without outlining it.

tween the outer and inner surfaces. Units composed of straight-edged shapes and curves painted onto the clay surface with a latex resist can be varied and repeated in concentric bands. The application of the glaze and the removal of the resist allow for a build-up of glaze which results in a low relief; the resist areas become slight depressions in the glazed surface.

A painted, two-dimensional circle can be designed to include the repetitious actions of figures, outlined to emphasize their individuality, outlined again to shadow the first contour, and outlined finally in a bold line for dramatic emphasis.

Black and White. Design by Gloria Perrino

Fabric design can utilize the circular form as pillows embroidered in a variety of stitches. Radiating lines and dots relate the decoration to the total form. Value contrast is advisable. Shapes may include both geometric and combined forms. Repeated line groupings provide detail and subject clarification. A batik based on concentric rings can vary its radial symmetry by alternating or varying the motif repeated within each radial band.

The essence of a particular medium and its technique may suggest a natural circular interpretation. The coiling technique used in some basketry follows concentric symmetry and can result in a circular structure. Macramé cords looped over a circular rim produce curved fiber lines which enhance the structure. The knot patterns of macramé may produce rounded nubs. Wax drops often occur in the batik process. The experienced designer effectively utilizes these drop shapes as a motif to be incorporated within the plan of the design. This drop is circular, although irregular in shape and, along with the dot, becomes a means of providing circular harmony and variety within the batik process. A U-shaped pattern unique to the woodworker's gouge tool is the result of the pressure exerted upon it, the shape of the gouge, and its placement upon a wooden surface. This "U" incorporates a curve and lends itself to the creation of texture that is harmonious to a circular shape.

Other materials, such as stones and beads, added to basic construction of a circular object should echo the circular form. In jewelry, the dominant shape of a pendant could create a countermovement to that of the encircling neck-fastening band. Attached materials, such as cords, can repeat the downward thrust. Long, straight needle attachments of metal can be melted at their ends, creating rounded orbs. A linear-relief design within the piece can incorporate negative arched shapes, with an ovoid negative space emphasizing the circular stone that provides the focal point of interest. A portion of the linear relief can outline and repeat the arched voids. The outer rim can be cut into, resulting in a notched edge. Detail interest can be provided by circles, dots, and scales as incised line. The repetition of similar units such as the arched form, alone or in combination, can provide interesting design possibilities for the circle.

A circular cloth form with negative circles cut away from it can be appliquéd onto a background cloth of a darker value for contrast. Simple geometric shapes can be appliquéd to the background within the "negative" spaces. A unifying machine-stitched line pattern can pull the units together.

A three-dimensional sculptured form can be rounded and incorporate the use of simple negative and positive circular shapes. The simplicity of a piece of sculpture can play up its roundness.

A round ceramic plaque with concentric, spaced rings reveals a curved, lumpy, free organic head within an inner ring. The head is in relief and protrudes out from the surface of the plaque. The bands are incised into the clay. Curved, three-dimensional finger forms jut out from the outer ring. Negative depressions create a textural field of interest.

Paper can be scored and folded to create relief patterns, incorporating radial spiraling with wrapping, overlapping, and flattening of shapes around a central core. Techniques appropriate to paper can be utilized to emphasize a circular theme.

The circle, as well as any other shape, can provide the shape for interpretation in any medium. Correlation of its parts will unify the whole.

Ceramic Relief Sculptured Disk. John Asquith. Collection, Dona Meilach

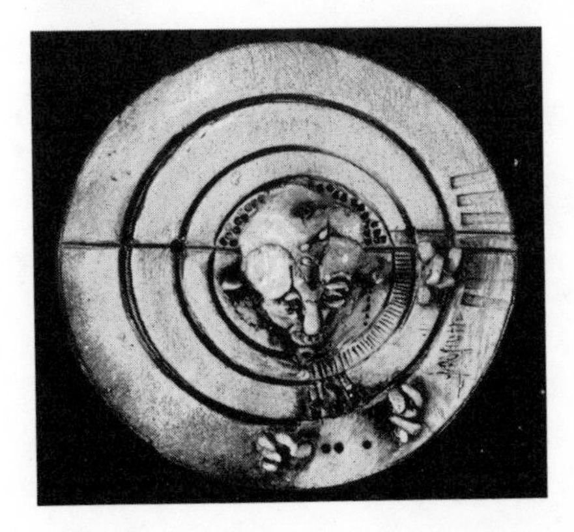

Paper Sculpture. D. Brown.
Student problem. Photographed at Illinois Institute of Technology. Institute of Design.

Paper Sculpture. Photographed at Illinois Institute of Technology. Institute of Design.

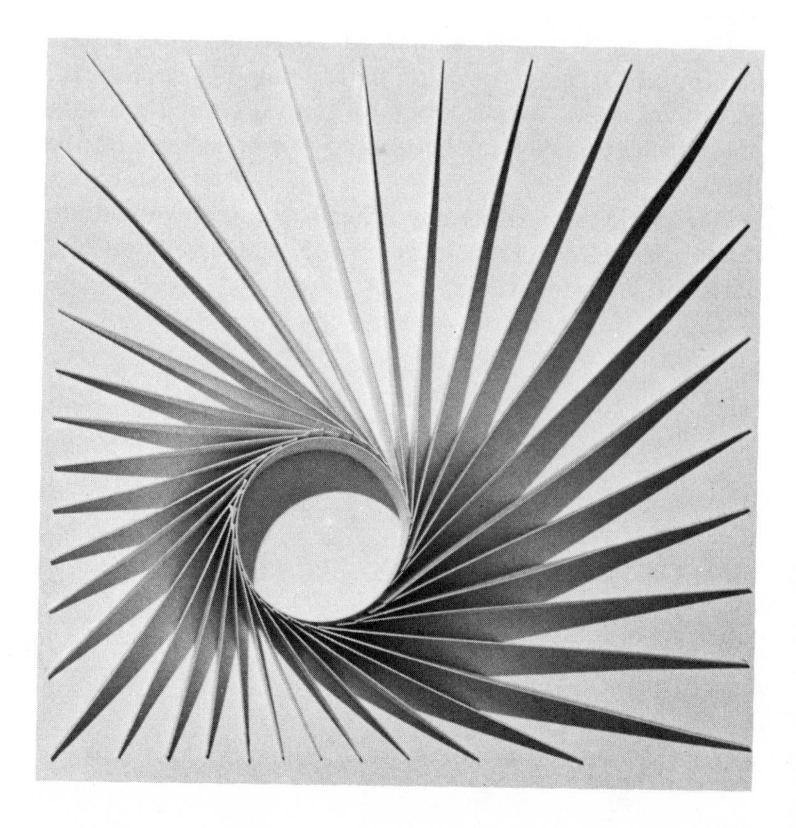

EXERCISES

Designing for a circle, square, triangle, rectangle, or any other specific shape has common problems. The design should conform to or suggest the space it is to fill. How can you apply the examples given in this chapter to designing for shapes other than the circle?

1. Design a square by breaking it up into simple straight-edged shapes of black, white, and gray.
   - A. Alter the values of the shapes.
   - B. Reverse the shapes as in a mirror image.
2. Design a rectangle by breaking it up into:
   - A. Triangles
   - B. Circles
   - C. Squares
   - D. Combinations of these.
3. Design an octagon by breaking it up into various triangles, being certain to include variation in value and/or size.
4. Select one particular shape and design six different ways to break up the space.

Simple Geometrics in black, white, and gray. Jay Hinz. Cut paper. Designed in multiple units for assembling and reassembling into several different arrangements.

CHAPTER 13

Sources and Interpretation

Four photographs, representing random patterns from natural sources, were carefully selected and submitted to several designers to illustrate how one source can provoke as many varied responses as there are interpreters. The result rests in how each individual analyzes and interprets the subject. Each artist's response reflects his education, experimentation, experience, and interest. All these add up to exposure which, in turn, equals conscious awareness. However, even if all had the same degree of awareness, the interpretations would still differ vastly. Why? Because throughout each person's development of judgment and choice, he has exercised certain positive responses. One person may prefer clean-cut, precise, symmetrical arrangements; another selects subtle, sketchy, asymmetrical arrangements. Some like vibrant colors; others elect soft, muted tones. And all interpretations are valid.

You are encouraged to study each of the four photographs and eventually make your own design from it for the medium of your choice. The following thought processes will help you understand how you can better develop an aesthetic interpretation. Armed with such an approach, you will be able to create designs that are exciting and unified and that embody the necessary elements and principles.

The first photograph for analysis is composed of *tree roots*. First, describe what you see immediately. Perhaps you will observe the gnarled, twisted writhing of three-dimensional linear forms. Then, think of all the words you can to describe what you see. For example, entangled, intermeshing, interweaving, intersecting, interpenetrating,

Pebbles. Bill Hinz. Negative photostat made from drawing based on photograph of "Pebbles," page 172.

Tree Roots. This photograph was presented to six artist/craftsmen for analysis and interpretation into any medium they chose. Study the following examples to see how each person extracted and used the portions they felt important.

winding, serpentine, meandering, random, overlapping, touching, extending, curved, vertical, diagonal, lateral, oblique, below, under, between, around, among, asymmetrical, recessed, connected, natural, organic, negative, positive. All these words help develop the theme. By consciously thinking the subject through and verbalizing the general character and movement of the piece, it should be easier to develop your idea visually into any medium.

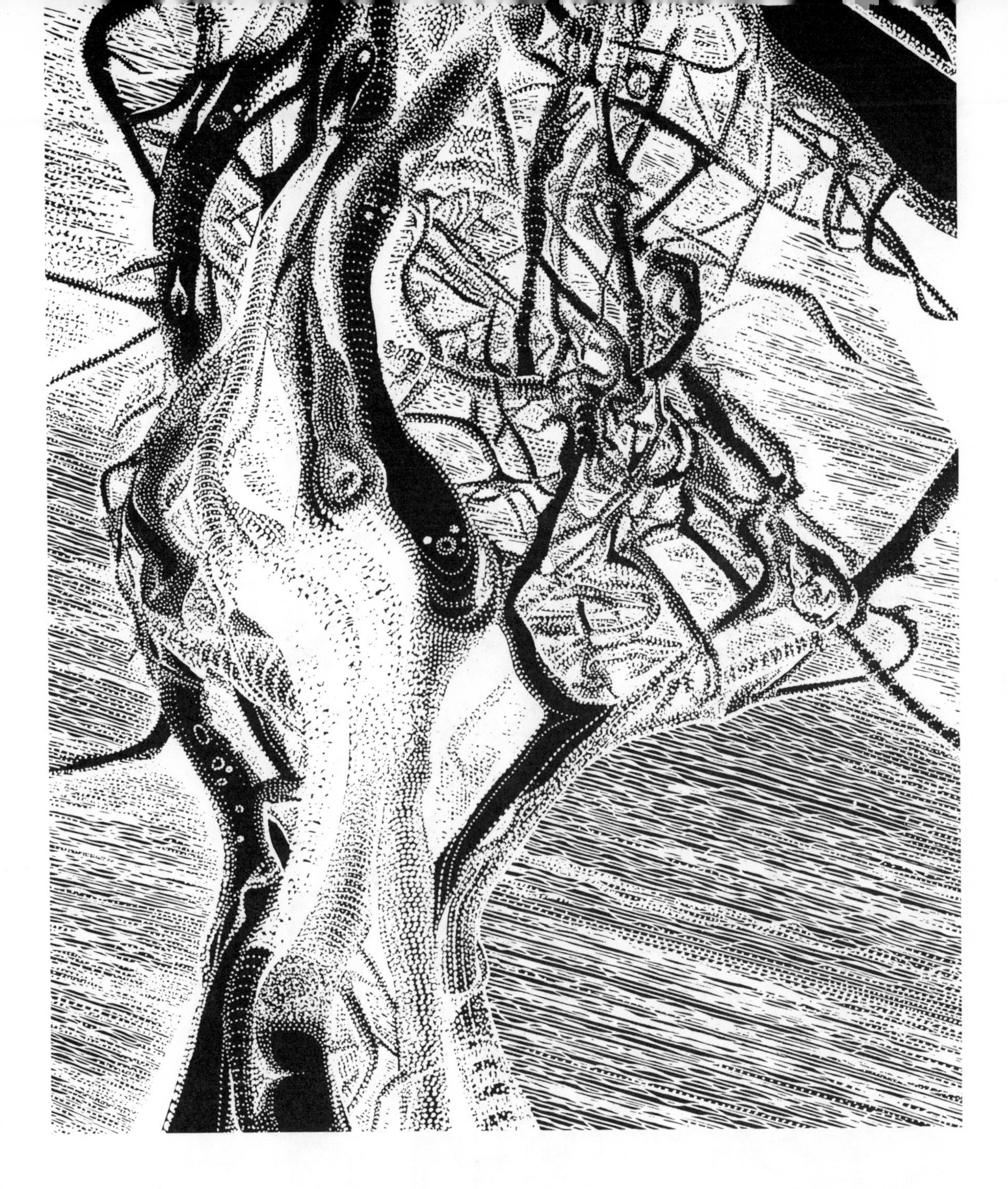

Let's ask questions and observe how the artists have interpreted these same root forms into various media. How do the designs differ to accommodate the materials from which they were made? What can a pen-and-ink drawing accomplish that a wrapped-cord-type construction cannot? What is inherent in the batik technique that will naturally develop a related texture? How were the design elements—dot, line, shape, texture and value—handled in each piece?

Tree of Life. Jay Hinz. Ink drawing.

Opposite:
Bill's Tree. Ink drawing, negative photostat.

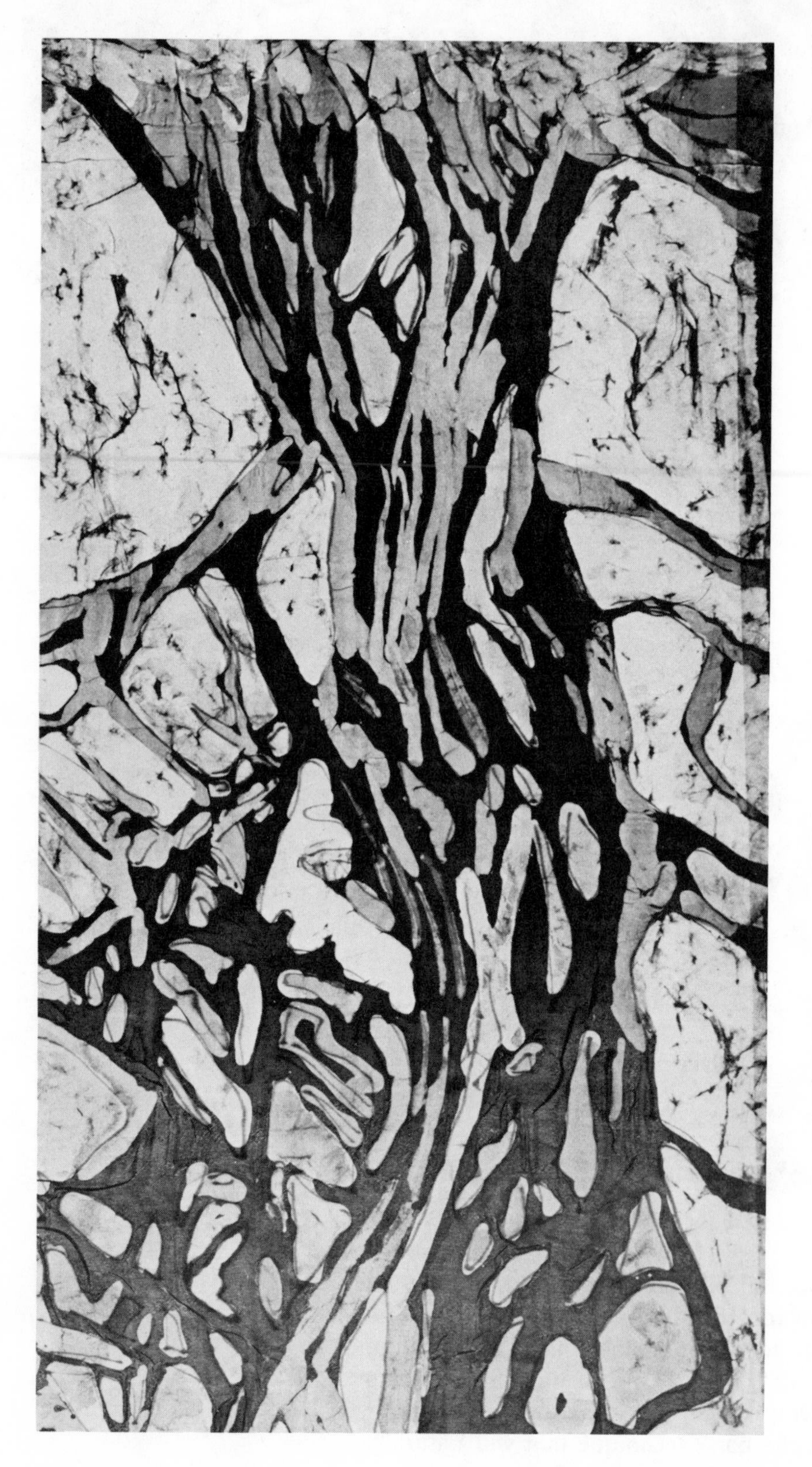

After the photo "Tree Roots." Judith Irany. Batik on silk.

Bill's Tree. (Detail of full tree-root interpretation, page 170) Bill Hinz. Ink drawing, negative photostat. This is a segment of the total drawing, turned upside down showing how a new point of view can create a new design.

Tree of Life. (Right) Jay Hinz. Ink drawing interpretation of "Tree Roots" photo, using dot and line for texture and value for two and three dimensional patterns.

(Interestingly, the only piece that employed color was the batik.)

The two dimensionality of batik and ink drawing made it necessary to rely on illusion to depict the third dimension. The photograph itself is a two-dimensional portrayal of the three-dimensional reality of tree roots. When working in two dimensions, it is possible to design a piece to "play up" the flatness. Another decision was whether or not to include the background of the photograph as a portion of the design. In the examples, the two-dimensional pieces did; the three-dimensional pieces did not. Background, or negative spaces, must always be equally considered along with foreground, or positive shapes, when designing for two dimensions. In a two-dimensional work, when materials used are different than the natural material, the artist must rely on textural interpretation. If a piece is designed for a relief carving, the three dimensionality of the background can be implied more easily than in a flat medium. In a three-dimensional fiber medium, the materials used can closely relate to those of the actual structure.

The second photograph illustrates nature's random scattering of pebbles. Shapes, textures, and values, emphasized by a rhythmical movement in natural balance, also assume additional interest through variation. Shapes change, sizes vary, values take on the extremes from black to white, with all of the subtleties of grays in between. The value patterns and the texture patterns become shape. The textures build up in density to alter the values. The elements of design are interdependent, overlapping, and interchangeable.

What words can describe this pebble picture? Small, medium, large, sharp, diffuse, dark, light, oval, irregular, spotty, random, scattered. What other relevant words can you think of? It is always helpful to look for contrasts; then, develop this contrast in your composition.

In the examples, the artists used the pebble photograph more as a "beginning" for improvisation rather than for a literal interpretation. Often designers use sources of inspiration only as a tool to get started and then discard them altogether. It is difficult, and unnecessary, to trace any similarity between the design and its source. The layman may feel ambiguity between the interpretation and its inspirational source, but he learns that all shapes may be borrowed.

The third photograph is of brain coral beneath the water's surface which offers swirling undulating patterns. Observe the nebulous, murky quality of some portions compared to precisely defined details of other areas. Notice the

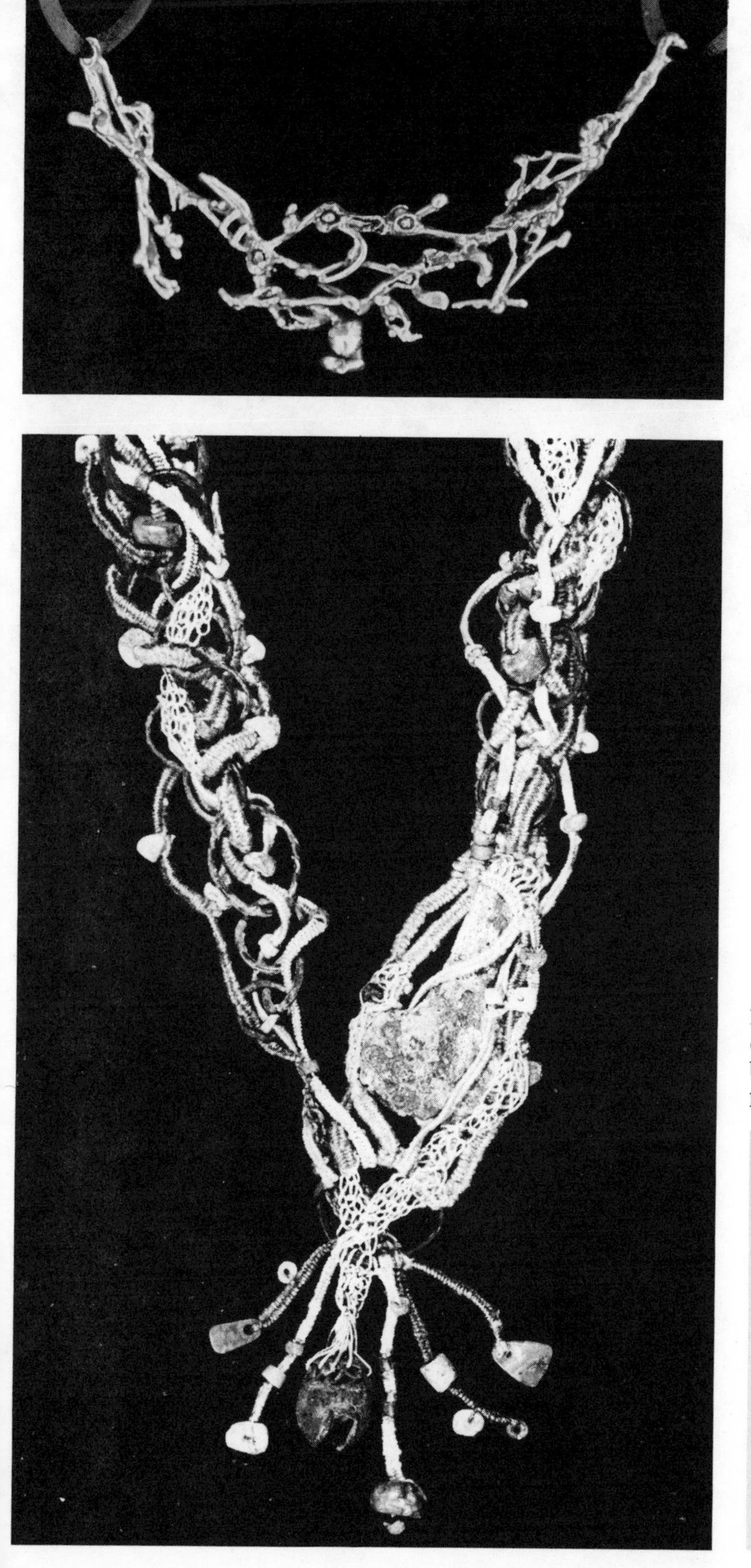

Bill's Tree. (Opposite) Bill Hinz. Ink drawing based on "Tree Roots" photo. Flat pattern. The tree roots are white and negative areas are black. Observe the various kinds of lines.

Root Form Necklace. Jil Kubica. Student, Hinsdale Central High School, Hinsdale, Illinois. Lost-wax process; cast in sterling silver.

Organic Necklace. Jane Chapman. Macramé with attached stones was inspired by an organic-root form. Courtesy, artist

Basket. Doris Hoover. Wrapped cord construction; could have been inspired by organic growth patterns.

Pebbles. A photo of pebbles on a beach was analyzed by Martha Underwood and Bill Hinz in the interpretations that follow.

small, circular bubbles that repeat throughout. Some appear to be only a small spot in places; in others they are white, ringed by a darker value. Some look relatively flat; others appear quite dimensional. The close coral ridges seem to spread out in some areas. As the value relationships play up some edges, they create shape. Locate subtle linear patterns and also notice the moiré effect the water suggests in the upper left-hand corner. Now begin to describe this photograph in words, as in the first three photos, so that you create a clear, mental picture using similarities, contrasts, and the words associated with design—line, point, shape, and so forth.

A detail from Eleanor Levine's batik simulates the water patterns. Other textural effects in the composition combine to emphasize an organic quality. This designer sums up her philosophy: "Rhythm, variety, repetition, balance, unity, harmony, direction are the principles of life, the principles of design, the principles of the design of life. I gather fragments of my own life and put them together—piece by piece—the parts that work for me are repeated. The less significant ones are minimized, changed, or elim-

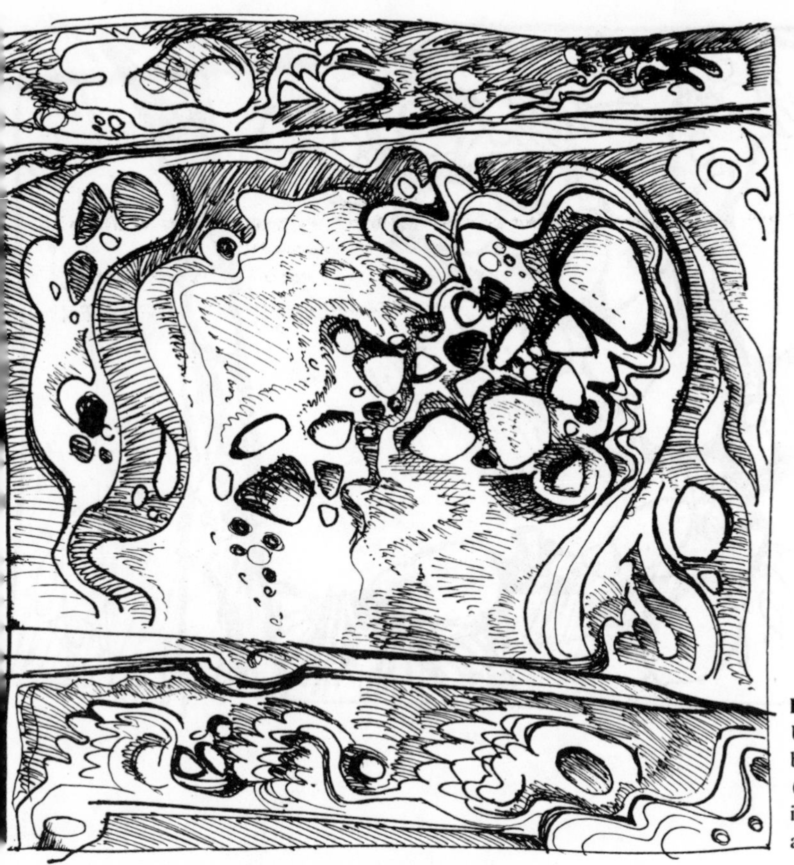

Pebble Design I. Martha Underwood. A quick ink sketch based on the photo "Pebbles" (opposite) will later be interpreted into a finished work in another medium.

inated. Many things are happening at once, in different areas, and I want to include them all. But when there is so much going on, it gets too busy. It is then necessary to tone down some areas and emphasize others. Vision is unlimited, yet there is a main theme. Sometimes I distract from, and other times I call attention to, the main theme—making it less important or giving it more weight—whichever it needs. Rhythm, born from the combination of opposites, finds its direction and creates unity, harmony, wholeness—a statement made for the moment."

"Fossils," by Virginia Bath, combines embroidery, bobbin, and needle-lace techniques using linen, wool, silk, rayon, wood, shells, and ceramic. She has carefully selected materials and methods which would capture the essence of the photograph. Subtle nuances exist between shapes, scale, movement, textures, and values with conscious control of arrangement and repetition. She has also consciously selected a support designed to be an integral part of the total design, a tree branch, whose shape and value provided a continuity of feeling. Every detail was designed to fit within the total structure—the negative areas, the free-hang-

Pebble Design II. Martha Underwood. Another ink sketch helps the artist further develop a pleasing composition.

Pebbles. Martha Underwood. Batik on silk. By making more than one quick sketch, the artist developed and expanded upon the concept, and the result is shown in her final batik. Courtesy, artist

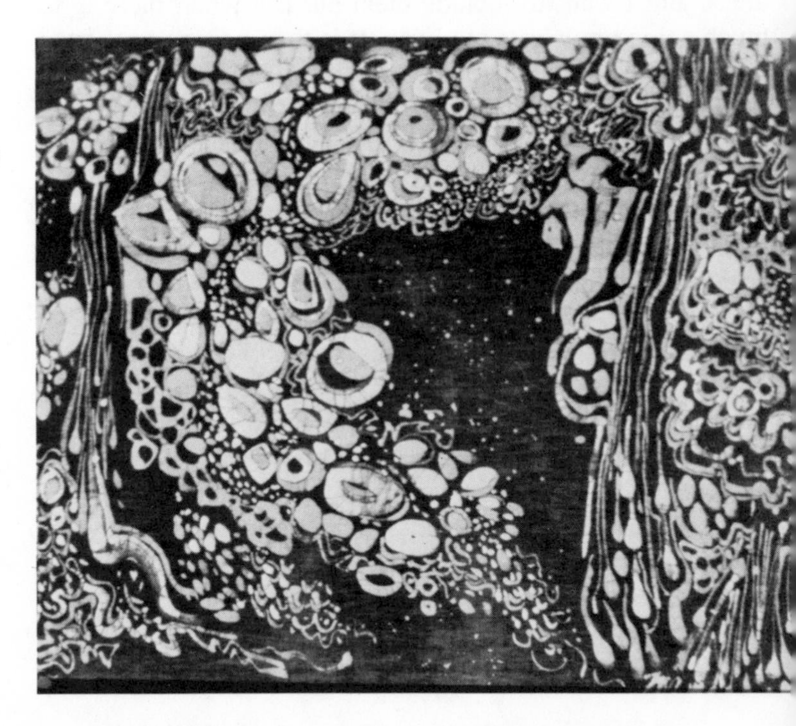

Pebble Theme. Bill Hinz. The original black-on-white ink drawing. Compare this with the negative photostat, page 162, purposely shown upside down for a different point of view.

Brain Coral. Another photograph analyzed by different artist/craftsmen, Eleanor Levine, Martha Underwood, Virginia Bath, and Bob Christiaansen, resulted in the interpretations that follow.

ing threads, the frugal, and thoughtful, addition of shells shells and ceramic beads.

Martha Underwood draws many preliminary sketches before she makes a final selection for her work. Her sketches are direct statements, ready for translation into the medium of her choice. From the brain coral she has isolated the repeated patterning of the lights, darks, and wormlike linear textures for her batik, using the natural hues of blue, turquoise, and white. Using the same source of inspiration, she created a more formal black, white, and gray pattern for her acrylic painting.

Bob Christiaansen was influenced by the textural qualities of the coral, as well as the light/dark relationship of shapes, to fashion a hammered-metal container. He capitalized on the reactions of light to a variety of surface depths to create the same undulating quality in metal as the coral under water.

The photograph titled "Natural Striation" is also organic, and an enlarged detail illustrates how one must look for a

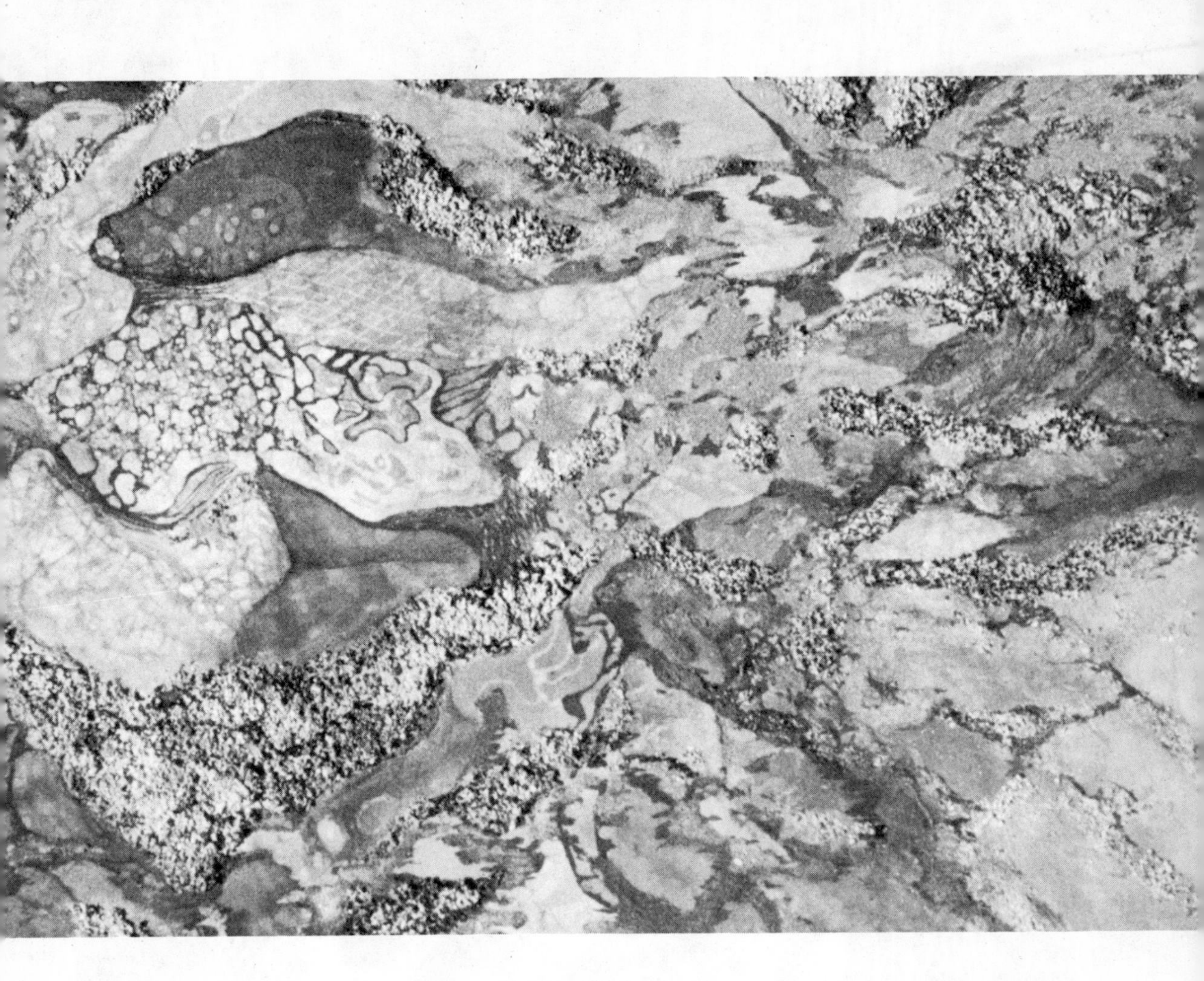

See Me, Feel Me, Know Me. (Detail) Eleanor Levine. Batik wax resist and overdye texture and patterning have the same elements and feeling as the organic brain coral. Courtesy, artist

general texture. For the purposes of design, it is not necessary to precisely identify it. It is more important to respond to what you see, without the prejudices that accompany absolute identification. How do you respond to the surface? How would you observe and describe it? Because nature has varied the regularity of the striae, you might use contrasting terms and consider variety versus regularity. Other opposites could be straight/angled; grooved/smooth; asymmetrical/symmetrical; parallel/opposed; dark/light; geometric edged/eroded, weathered, decayed edge; organic/artificial; linear/massive; amorphous/stratification. Then consider similarities such as calcified-hard-stony; soft-spongy-flexible. Other descriptive words relevant to this structure are minute grooves, channels, threadlike lines, narrow bands, streaks, stripes, series of parallel lines, textures. The direction or movement as well as the patterning of the darks and lights also play an important role in the total impact.

In interpreting this photograph, the batik captured the over-all effect of the value arrangement and the feeling of

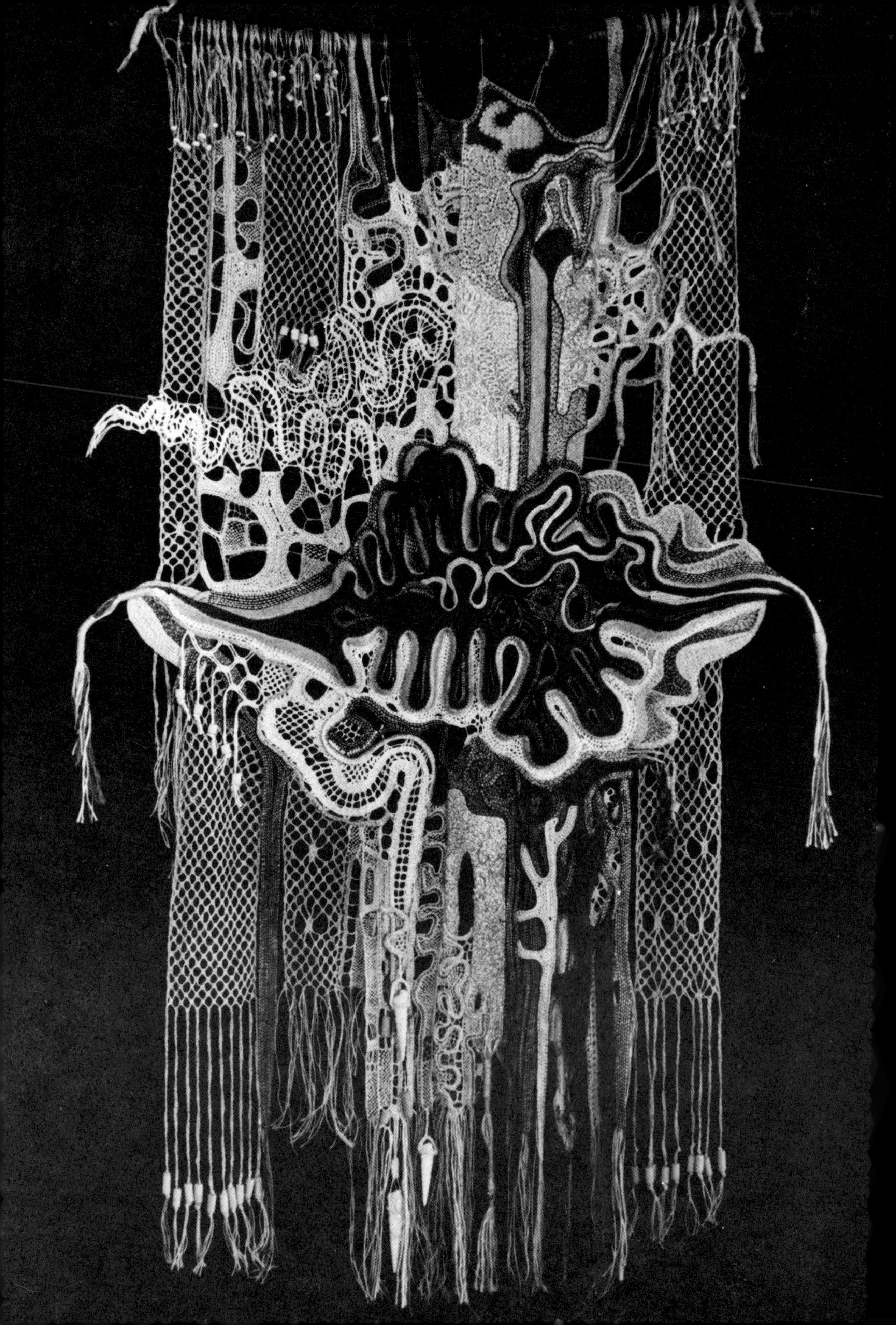

Fossils. (Opposite) Virginia Bath. 1972. 28″ wide, 48″ high. Embroidery, bobbin, and needle-lace techniques using linen, wool, silk, rayon, wood, shells, and ceramic. The entire composition was inspired by the photo "Brain Coral." (See details, below.) Courtesy, artist

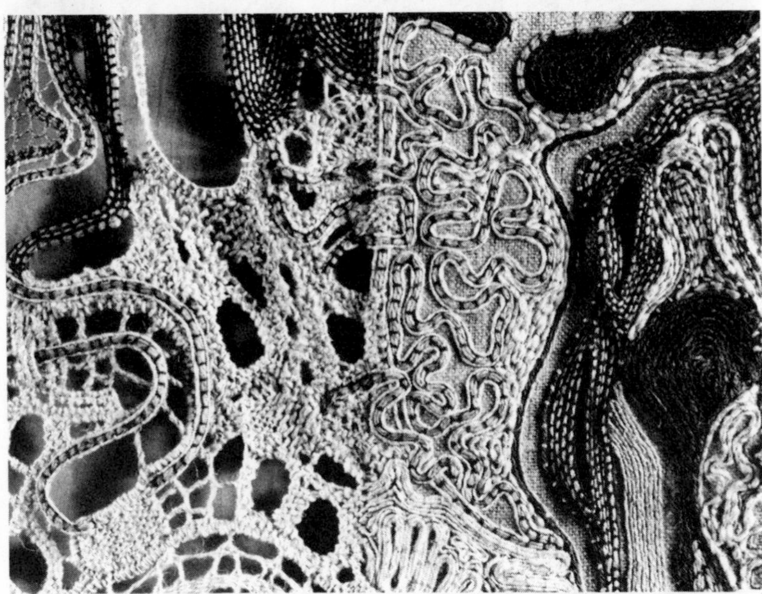

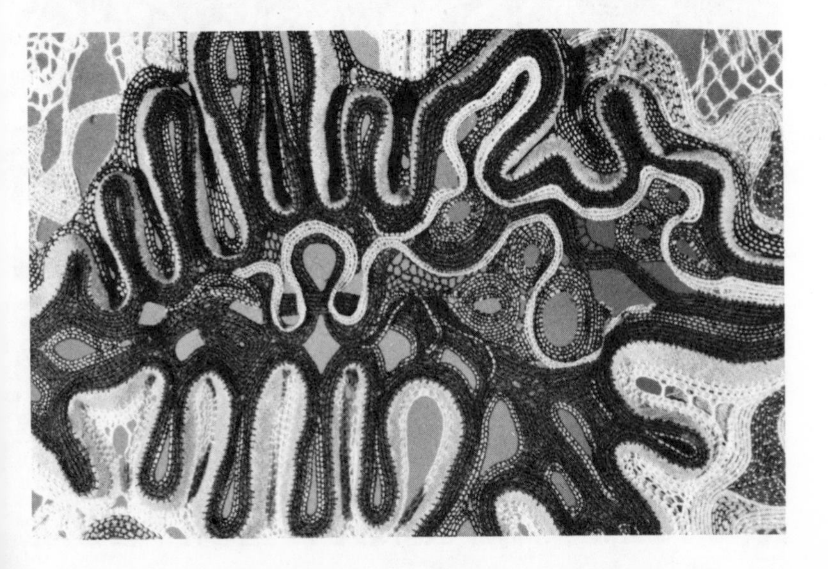

Details of the composition "Fossils." Virginia Bath. Each could become a separate composition if desired.

Top photo shows the upper-central portion.

Middle photo shows the detailing in the upper-left section.

Bottom photo is a detail of the central portion. Photos, courtesy artist

Brain Coral Drawings. Martha Underwood. Two quick pen sketches help her extract essential components to use for her final design in batik, below.

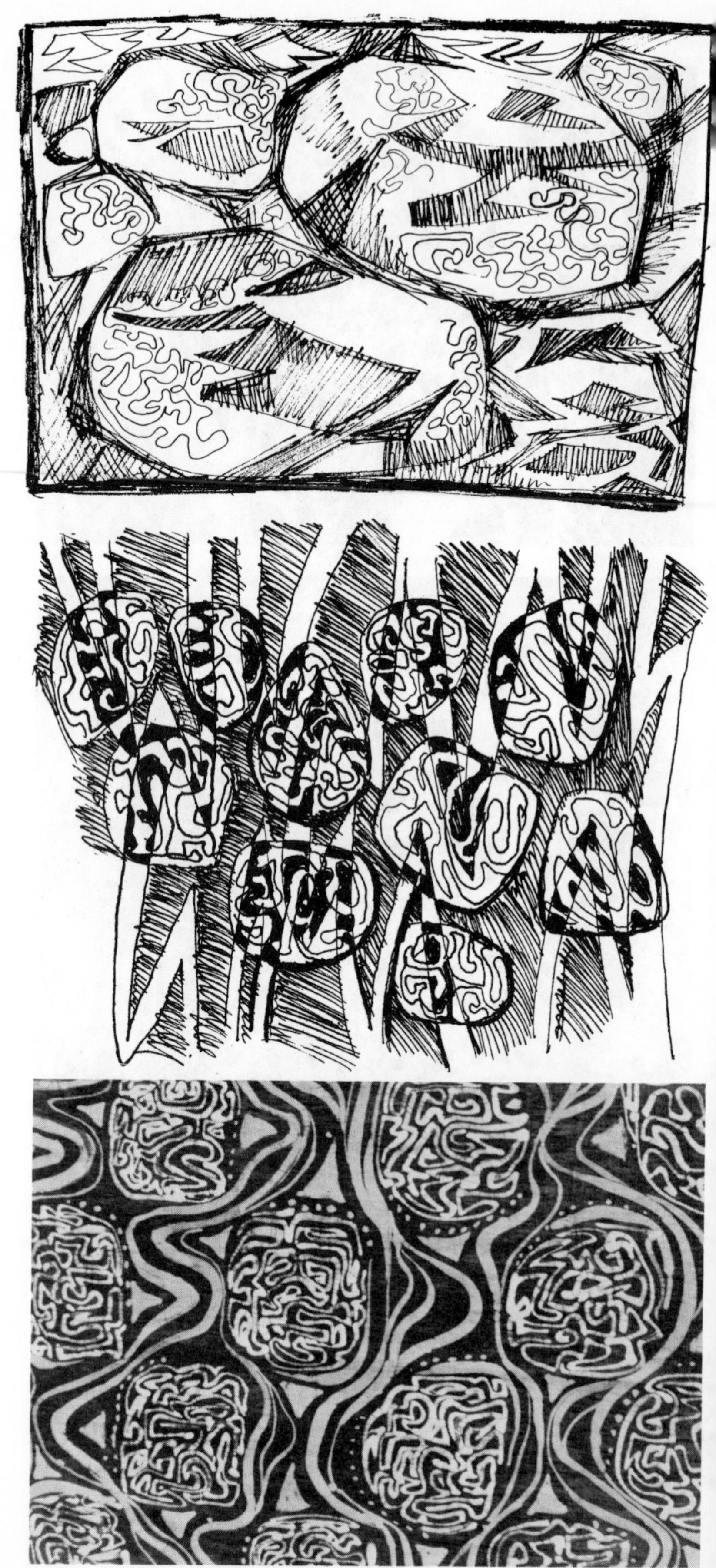

Brain Coral. Martha Underwood. Batik. 32½″ high, 42″ wide. Blue, turquoise, and white. The final batik design was interpreted into a more uniform arrangement of shapes held together by the flowing linear movement and the value relationships. The characteristic "wormlike" line pattern of coral is a negative design in the all-over dark, continuous shape. Courtesy, artist

dots and sketchy ridges, although in some portions the values were reversed. The crackle added its own character to the piece.

Both collages treated the subject similarly; Marion Hall's collage using wood veneers results in a more literal translation than Elvie Ten Hoor's paper collage. The inherent texturing of the wood has much of the same quality as that in the source photograph while the paper employs torn edges to create the illusion of the texture.

Jane Knight developed a three-dimensional crochet inspired by an oval detailed section isolated from the central portion of the photograph. The other elements—the band of contrast, the top ringlike structures, and the texture—

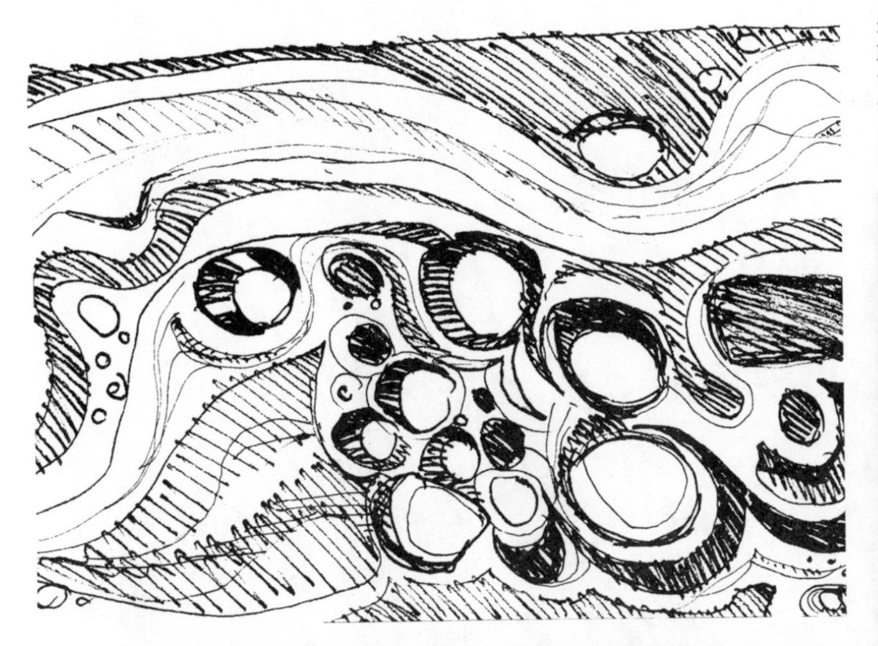

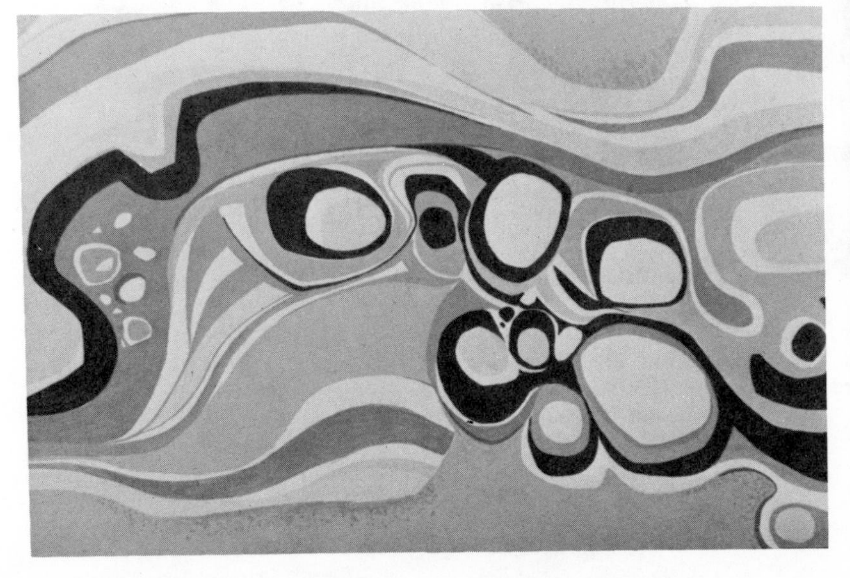

Another sketch derived from analysis of the "Brain Coral" photo was developed into the acrylic painting below, left, by Martha Underwood. Courtesy, artist

Vase. Bob Christiaansen. An interpretation of brain coral in hammered copper has an undulating surface and dot texture in a medium that differs from flat pattern on paper or fabric.

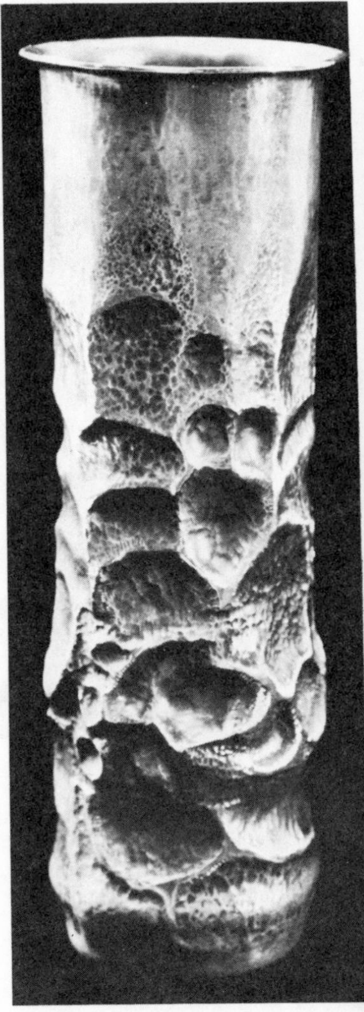

Natural Striation. A close-up detail photo of an unidentified subject was analyzed and interpreted by Blanche Carstenson, Elvie Ten Hoor, Marion Hall, Jane Knight, Leora Stewart, Bill Hinz, and Jay Hinz in their chosen media.

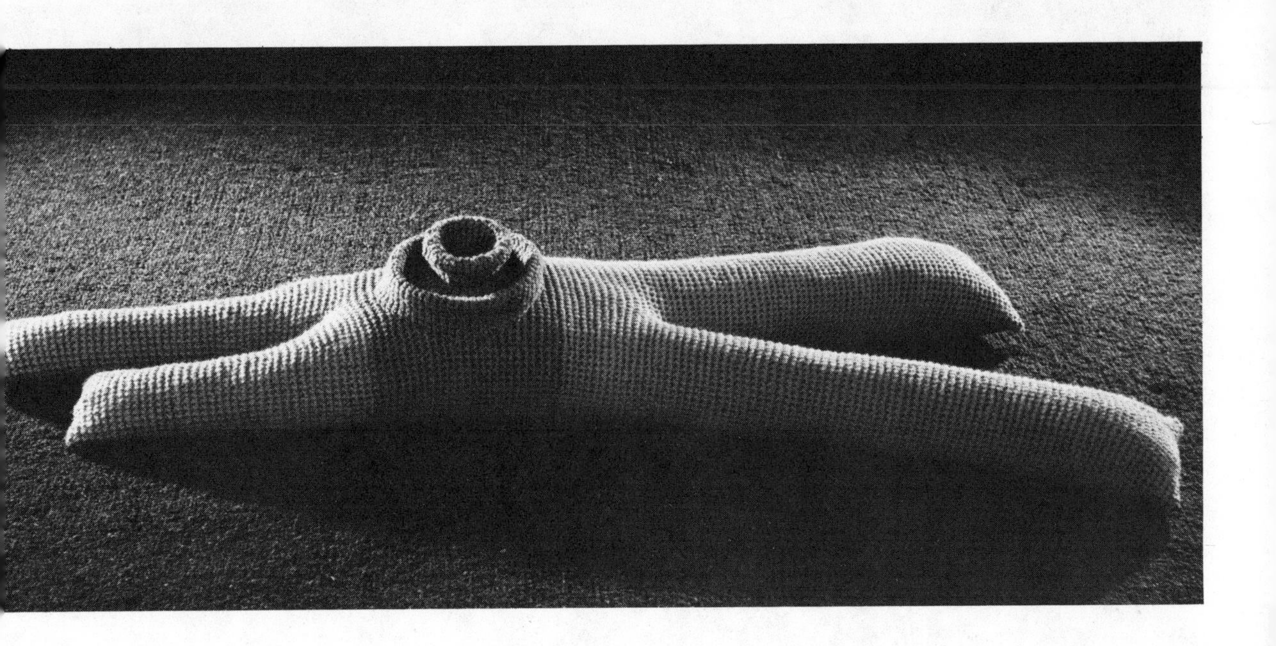

represent her creative response and choice for integrating detail with over-all form.

Leora Stewart's fiber sculpture adapted the negative, linear, dark-valued rift to become the deep space surrounding the vertical core of her wrapped and knotted yarns. She says, "It is not only the texture, but the whole shape that is encompassed in the photo that I like—the feeling of a form that has edges that are soft and fuzzy, and the structure beneath being sturdy—the wrapping in the piece in black and white wool relating to the black and white shadows in the photo—it feels similar in spirit."

Crochet Form. Jane Knight. A stuffed, three-dimensional crochet was inspired by the portion shown below of the "Natural Striation" photograph. Photo, Richard Knight

Natural Striation. An ovoid area is isolated as the point of interest for Jane Knight's knitted form.

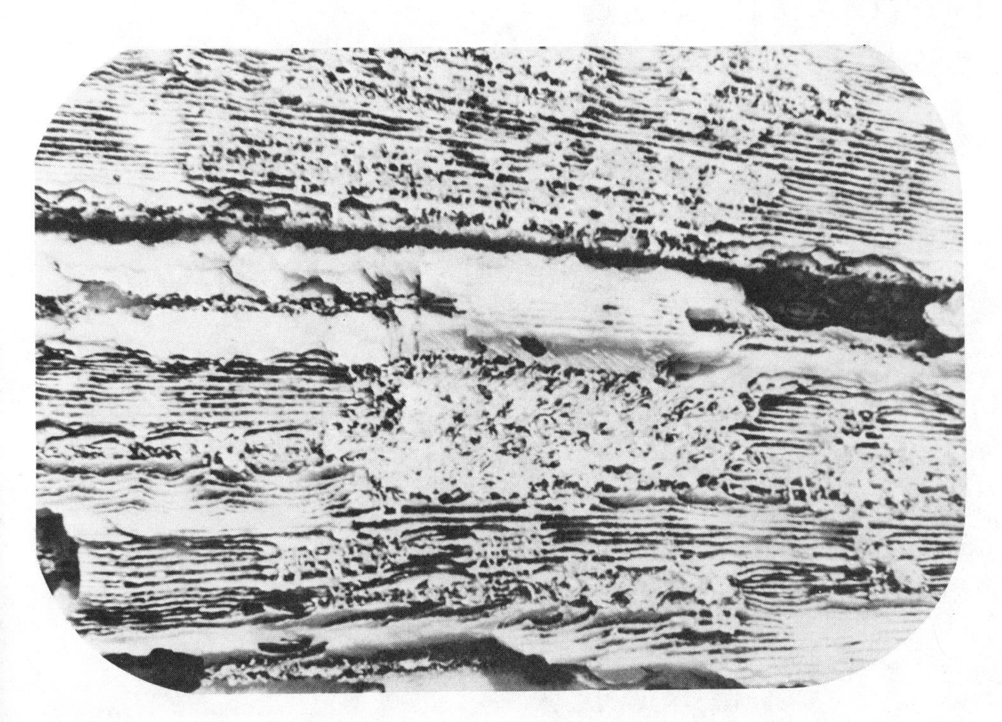

Axum. (Opposite) Leora K. Stewart. 5′ high, 26″ all around. Natural jute and black and white wool. Knotted core and wrapped threads with unraveled end threads cut and shaped. Miss Stewart's interpretation of the photo "Natural Striation" already existed in a recently created piece. The wrapping in black and white relates to the black and white shadows in the photo. Courtesy, artist

Axum. (Detail) Leora K. Stewart. The same central vertical thrust and adjacent verticals and horizontals that exist in the organic photo exist in the fiber sculpture. The feeling of a form that has edges which are soft and fuzzy, with the structure beneath being sturdy. Courtesy, artist

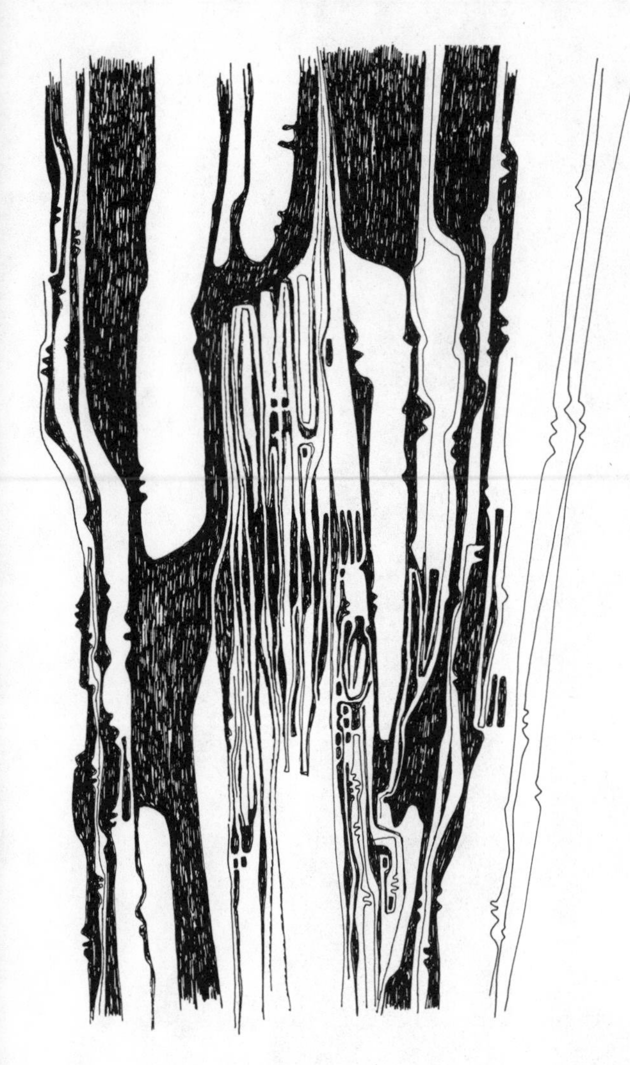

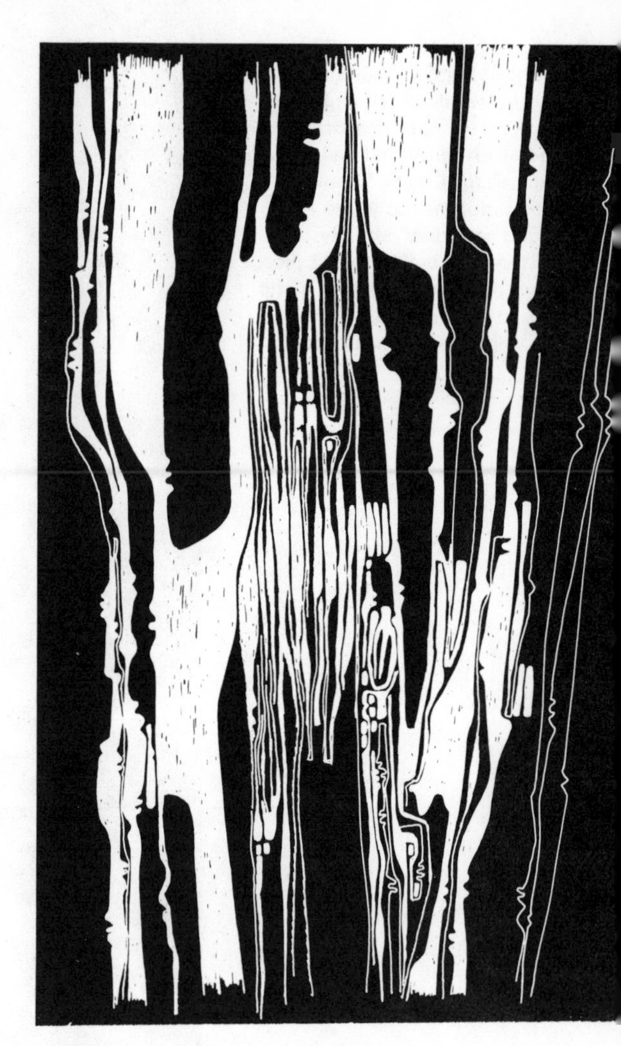

Striation. Bill Hinz. Ink drawing interpretation of the photo titled "Natural Striation."
(Left) Negative photostat.
(Right) Positive photostat.

In the ink drawings both interpretations were made from the photograph in its entirety. "Variation," composed entirely of dots, is more detailed than "Striation." The varied densities create variation in values. The general break-up of space is similar to the photograph. "Striation" is bolder and composed of strong, linear statements. The value areas are built up with linear strokes of the pen which create textural interest. Note that in "Variation," the open area occurs precisely where the most densely detailed area appears in "Striation." *Individual interpretations from the same source!*

Once you have created a design, it too can lead to additional sources for inspiration. A negative image of your own design can produce an entirely different feeling from the positive. To use this stimulating reversal concept as a tool, you will have to have your work photostated. The

process involves making a negative from the positive—the same negative from which the printer makes the positive. This negative can be exciting; it is also possible to have your work blown up or reduced in dimension by the same photostatic means. An 8″×10″ work can be expanded to 32″×40″ or larger, or diminished to 2″×2½″ or sizes in between.

Another approach using the photostatic process is to have an extra copy made of your design. Cut it apart, and carefully preserve the sheet from which the positive shapes have been cut. Each piece can be considered as a separate design. Since these are pieces, maneuver them freely until you assemble them into a composition that best pleases your aesthetic judgment. Glue them down. There should be little recognition between the "new" and the original composition. The sheet with the negative spaces provides another design, or it can be the start of a new one.

Variation. Jay Hinz. Ink drawing interpretation of the photo titled "Natural Striation."
(Left) Positive photostat.
(Right) Negative photostat.

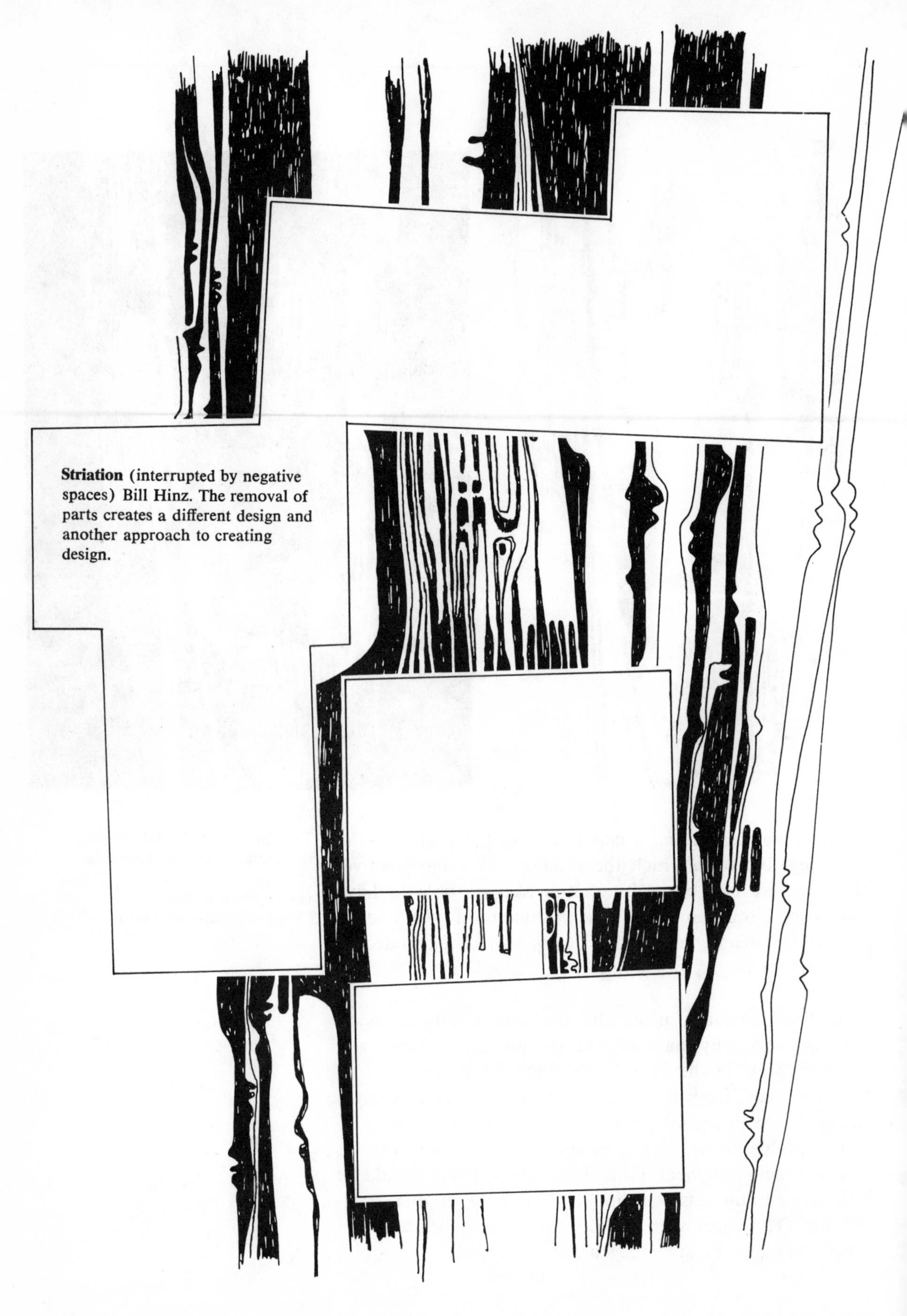

Striation (interrupted by negative spaces) Bill Hinz. The removal of parts creates a different design and another approach to creating design.

Striation-Assembly. Bill Hinz. The individual cutout parts can suggest new, individual designs. But they can also be repositioned in the cutout areas for different effects. You might photocopy these pages, cut out the parts, and reassemble them in various positions. Then try the same exercise with your own designs. Use the following photos to inspire your designs.

Mabel Hutchinson emphasizes her method for applying design principles to her wood constructions in which each piece must be related and support another, giving strength and structure. (See color photo page 135.) She says, "I never sketch a panel, or preconceive a design. My designs are dictated by the wood pieces that fill my studio." Her husband uses many rare hardwoods—rosewood, teak, zebra, walnut, maple, ash—and many other exotic woods to create furniture. The pieces that fall to the floor are her media for unique doors and panels.

Mrs. Hutchinson's challenge is to build order out of chaos. She begins with a blank piece of plywood and then, "I dump out a box of blocks and begin sorting and shifting them in all directions . . . I rely upon the vertical and horizontal line to bring order and consistency to the wholeness . . . I strive to carry throughout a certain linkage of line and curve and rounds. I repeat textures and shapes to create wholeness. To maintain continuity throughout a large area, I work toward a repetition of line and curve to pick up a movement and join these for integration and consistency. I am constantly aware of the pitfall of the obvious. I strive to create surprises . . . to deviate from the old principles without losing sight of them. Texture is fascinating and can bring interest into the designs. I enjoy the highly polished piece of rosewood next to a block of walnut filled with checks, bark, and uneven edges. The stark contrast creates surprises. The true character of wood can be exploited for interest and beauty. I would not throw any piece of wood away because of shape or texture. I can find a place for it, no matter how small or grotesque. I find the most beautiful wood grain next to the knots and burls, which is the part most likely to be thrown away. These are the wood pieces I exploit. Color, contrast, and values grow out of my woods. The only stain that I use is charcoal rez as a sealer and stain for background. Occasionally I will lightly stain a block when it has a tendency to jump out of the composition. I spend hours on sanding and oiling and, finally, I wax and polish."

The apparent spontaneity of Mabel Hutchinson's designing technique is in reality based upon many years of study and experimentation. Although the pieces seemingly fall into place without thought, actually designing is a conscious act that is intimately bound up with the emotional and mental responses directly related to the individual's education, exposure, and experience.

All creative techniques involve craftsmanship. Some techniques are more time-consuming than others. Care and

A composition created in clay relies on impressions from natural and man-made objects. Portions of this composition could be extracted and used for design inspiration in other media.

patience are necessary commodities. Comparative time involvements are only discovered through experience. In the case of the dedicated designer, it is improbable that time involvement enters into the selection of the medium.

With the necessary interest and effort, with continued direction toward finding beauty in the ordinary, recognizing the potential in every source of contact, and applying the elements and principles of design to each interpretation, *everyone can create good design.*

Bird-of-Paradise.

Base of Pinecone on Wood.

Wood.

EXERCISES

1 Use the photo of "Bird-of-Paradise" (page 194) as inspiration. Create a design resembling the shapes, directions and placement angles, and value arrangement in the photograph as closely as possible.

2 Refer to the photo of "Brain Coral" (page 176). Take any portion of the photograph and interpret it into a design. Notice the dark value and shapes the shadows create and that the light shapes are effective because of the amount of contrast between the values of the adjacent shapes.

3 Refer to the photo of "Wood." Use the entire photograph as inspiration for your design. Eliminate what you consider unimportant to the design. Emphasize portions you wish to bring out. Play up the asymmetrical balance within this composition.

4 Use the photo of "Cactus Needles" as a springboard for an idea for a design for stitchery. How could the linear needles be interpreted into embroidery stitches?

Be certain to include contrasting lines and textures, shapes and values, and balance all of them within your compositions. Any one of these problems can be interpreted so as to fulfill the design requirements for a specific medium. These designs can also be transposed from black, white, and gray into colors of the same value. The colors selected may be literal or imaginary. Each design you do can provide the starting point for improvisation and additional new designs. Each idea can be executed several times with a different subtle change each time.

Cactus Needles.

CHAPTER 14

Design Approaches

Approaches to design are unlimited if you are aware of them. Developing awareness through a conscious use of all of your senses will alert you to many inspirational avenues. Leaf, weed, and branch forms may be inked and printed once or many times to alter the direction of the lines and textures. You can imitate these prints from nature's objects to create a design in any medium. An effective, creative silk-screen print can be produced on a material other than fabric or paper. Acetate, for one, provides interesting possibilities because of its qualities of transparency, durability, and washability.

When you begin to design, first determine the subject and format size, then select any of various materials, such as oil pastels, colored pencils, or marking pens, to create a spontaneous initial design. The process you are designing for may dictate the best medium. For example, if you were designing a hooked rug, available yarn colors should be selected first. Match the colors as closely as possible with oil pastels, colored pencils, or marking pens; or match them perfectly with designer's gouache or acrylic paints.

When designing directly, you will learn to develop line, shape, value, and color. If the total does not come easily, try to develop a line drawing first, in pencil or ink, to determine the subject or develop the idea, perhaps a family of figures, or an African-inspired primitive. The line drawing may then be interpretated into shape and value and finally be transposed into colors with corresponding values. It is then transferred to the working material in the size and scale required.

A piece can be designed in several component parts as shown in "African Primitive" (page 205). These parts

Leaves. Elenhank Designers, Inc. Inking leaves and overprinting them on acetate results in a repeat design which can be used for fabrics and wallpapers.

Tokara. Elenhank Designers, Inc. 58″ repeat. Two 46″ widths of fabric are joined together. One width shows the design used flat for wallcovering, the other is folded as drapery. The design was developed using the pressed-oil technique described on page 199. Courtesy, artists

can be mounted and viewed independently, or in combination. To be effective when viewed together, the units can be designed to fit as a continuous unit. All the vertical and horizontal sides may be designed to interconnect. It is possible to integrate lines and shapes by connecting extending points from one edge to the other or others and maintain the same character of line, shape, texture, value, and color relationships in each component piece. When enlarging and transferring the design onto burlap or canvas, the points of contact should be checked to be certain they coincide.

To stimulate design ideas, you may research a particular subject such as a bird or insects. Their lines, shapes, textures, and colors can provide inspiration for scores of designs. You might want to quickly sketch the subject as you see it in your yard, at a museum or at the zoo, or draw portions from book illustrations and magazines.

Another design approach is to work "in the style" of a particular phase of art history such as Byzantine or Cubism. Isolate the main characteristics of the style and develop your design within this structure. One design usually evolves from another.

Sometimes something we see or do inspires design. The peeled paint on an old barn is a favorite inspiration for painters, collage artists, and photographers. Often design begins with a doodle. Whether sketching casually; drawing deliberate shapes; cutting paper shapes; folding paper and cutting into it, or dipping it into dye for pattern; rolling or

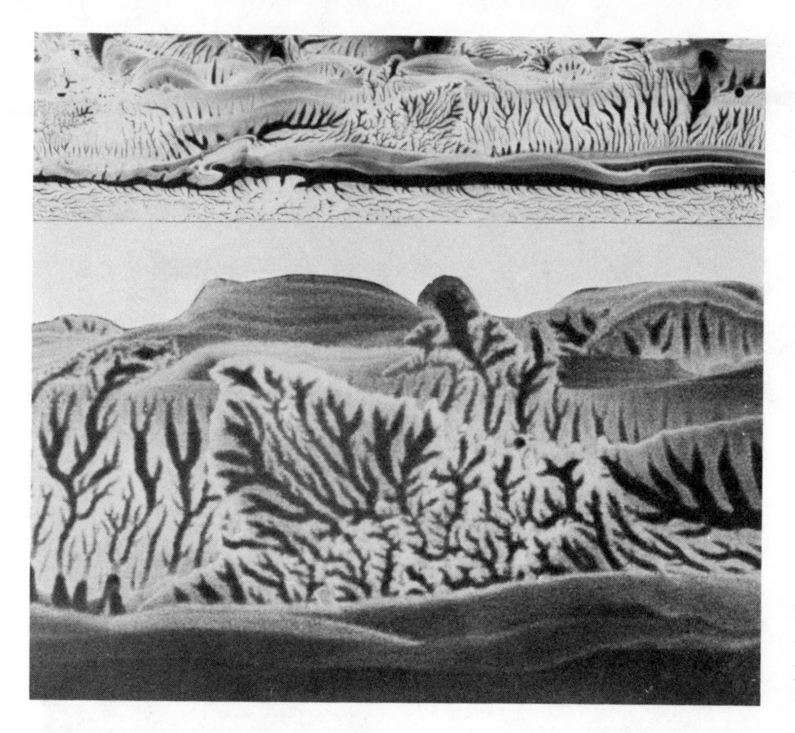

Tokara (designs for). Elenhank Designers, Inc. Original pressed-oil print on paper and a blown-up detail, below.

pressing various pigments; printing from nature forms; using pencil, ink, or any other medium, the result will be a design. The material and technique used will be your choice.

Pressed-oil and pressed-starch paint methods create intriguing patterns that can suggest fantastic landscapes and myriad other ideas. In the oil technique, a variety of oil colors are brushed onto a thin sheet of cardboard. This cardboard is pressed onto a sheet of paper with a flexible, rolling motion, starting at the top of the cardboard and lifting off the bottom. Pressed-starch paint is made by mixing two tablespoons of cornstarch with two tablespoons of cold water to which is added one cup of boiling water. This mixture is brought to a boil while stirring constantly. Powdered batik dyes or acrylic paints may be added to the cooled mixture. The colors are printed the same way as with the oil paints. Any portion of the resulting print can be enlarged and perfected to result in the silk-screen fabric pattern illustrated by Elenhank. The same pattern appears differently when the fabric is draped than when it is flat.

A well-designed unit may be adapted to any two-dimensional or low-relief sculpture medium including: mosaic; plaster or wood relief; piece of jewelry; batiked, block-printed, direct-dyed, hooked, or silk-screened fabric; acrylic, egg tempera, or oil painting; an ink drawing, or a print. Some designs are adaptable as surface decorations on three-dimensional objects such as ceramics, wood, or stone.

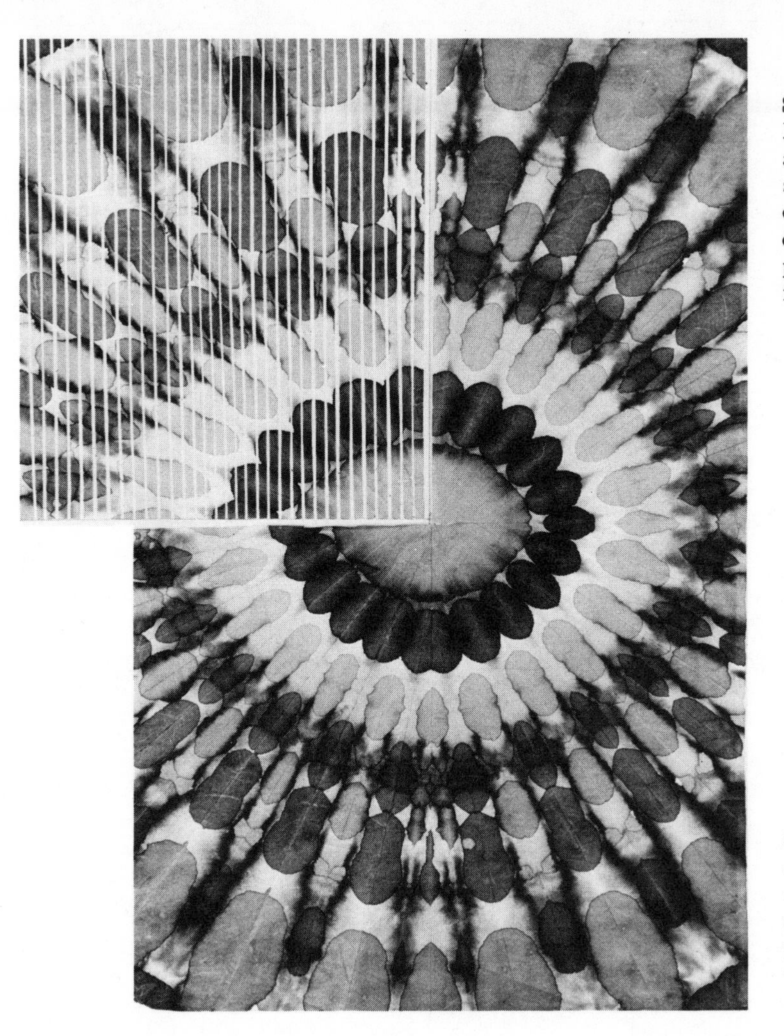

Solar. (Opposite) Elenhank Designers, Inc. 7′ high by approximately 8′ wide. A supergraphic-mural print for drapery and wallcovering was developed from half of a fold-dye paper design. A marvelous source for repeat pattern.

Solar. (Original fold-and-dye design inspiration) The inset shows a "blow up" of a quarter of the pattern. The silk-screened print at left is based on one-half of the pattern and embellished with added line and texture.

These designs may utilize full color, or they can be interpreted in value only, as in ink, engraving and etching, or carved relief. Each value could be represented by a change in level; the lowest level could represent the darkest value.

Some design techniques adapt more readily to specific art forms. A metal assemblage and a stained-glass window may be designed by the same method. First create a line pattern; within the lines, plan a balance of colored shapes. The line may be replaced by metal strips, or other hard material of collage, or by leading used with stained glass. Inner shapes may be replaced by metal or glass pieces. The different colors can be interpreted with different metals or by various treatments on the metal such as patinas produced with acids or weathering.

If you are designing for needlepoint, it is best to work directly on graph paper, using a different symbol to represent each color. Each mark represents one stitch.

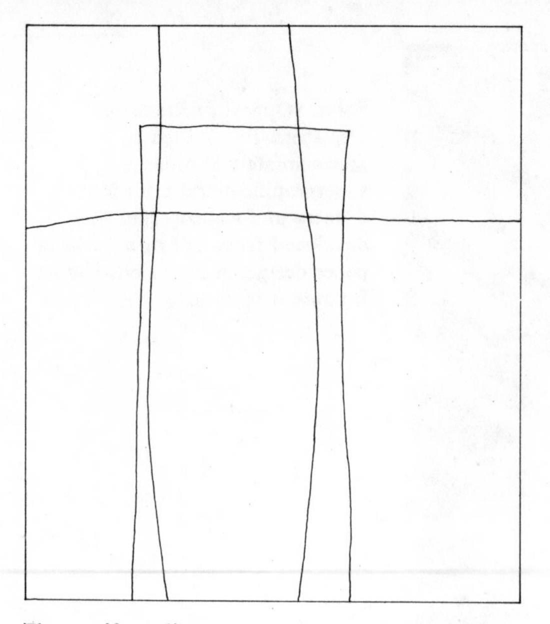

Fine, uniform line.

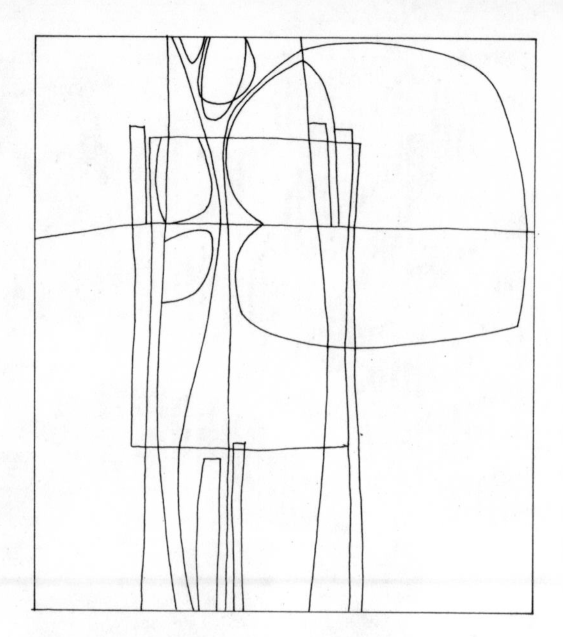

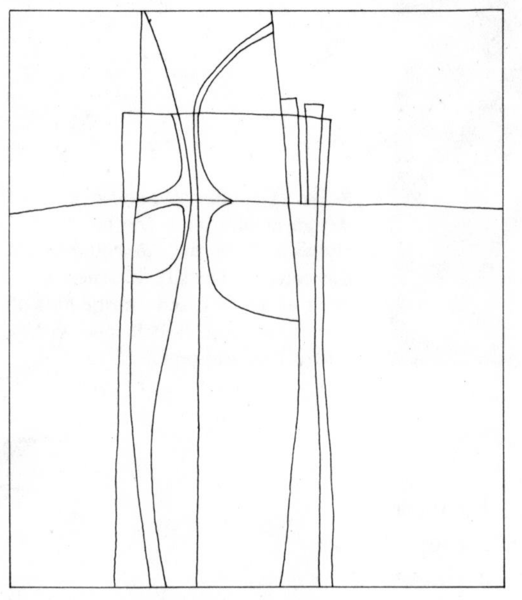

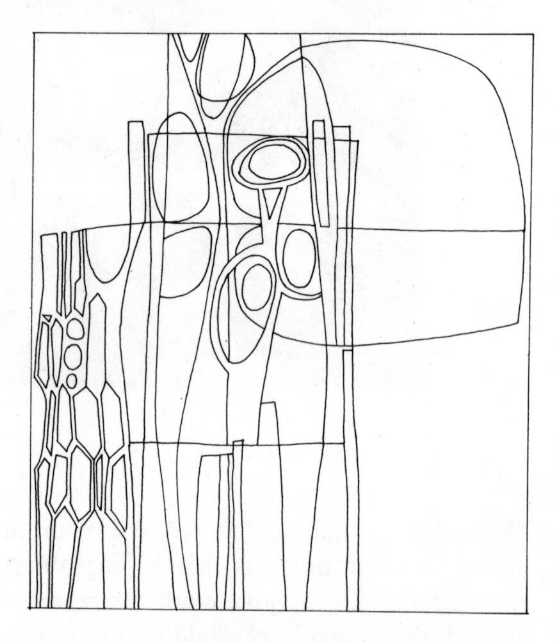

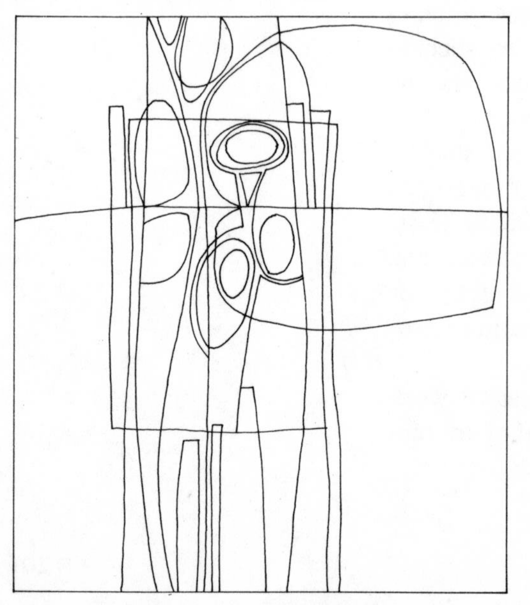

The Development of a Design.
Bill Hinz. Ink drawing.

Thick and thin line, brush-stroke texture.

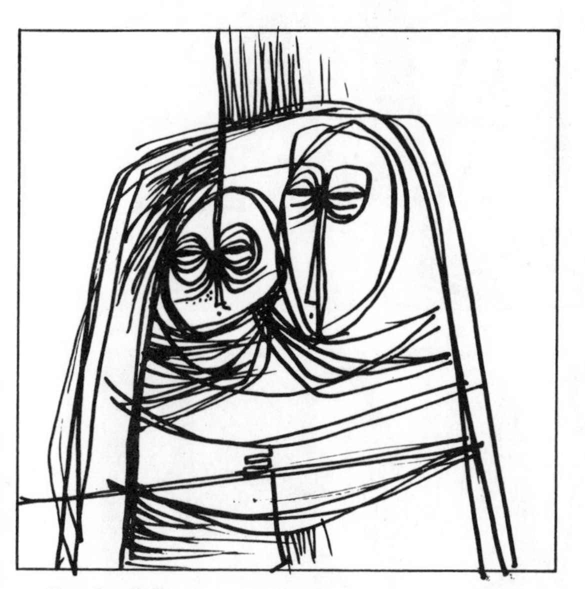

Sketchy line.

Textures.

Design Variations on a Theme.
Bill Hinz. Ink drawing.

Another inspiration for design is offered by the contrast between the black and white keys of a piano keyboard and the arrangement of them in relationship to each other. In the example titled "Piano Keyboard," instead of maintaining the "reality" of the static uniformity of the keyboard, several keyboards were designed in bands, each band becoming an interesting shape in itself. Every pattern of black, white, and gray balances individually, as do all of them totally. The emphasis was shifted from the keyboard to include a face and a bottle. See page 211.

Beginning with the keyboard idea, other subjects can be added, but the total must be unified through the elements and principles of design. Other musical instruments and

African Primitive. (Opposite) Jay Hinz. Colored-pastel pencil rendering. The composition is actually two panels split through the center to provide two units designed to be used separately or to fit together left to right, right to left, top to bottom, and bottom to top.
(Left below) Side-by-side, contact arrangement.
(Right) The same two units, one on top of the other, results in one long vertical panel. These designs were created for a hooked rug wall panel with the versatility of size and space rearrangement.

Family. Jay Hinz. Ink developmental sketch. The darkest values are determined at this stage of the sketch.

Family. Jay Hinz. Designer's gouache-colored rendering in warm pinks, beiges, and rusts. By adding the middle-value colors, grays in the photograph, the shapes between the lines, and the negative white spaces become more prominent. This design was developed into a Persian wool hooked wall hanging.

musicians can offer design inspiration; Picasso's "The Three Musicians" and Braque's cubist still lifes with violins, guitars, and other instruments are prime examples. You must develop the ability to see the possibility in a subject and be willing to play with interpreting it as a design. You must be able to experiment beyond known visual relationships. If a keyboard looks straight-edged, you should be willing to try it with a curve.

Bimorphic, interlocking shapes are another design potential. A single contour can become a common line shared between a bird on one side and an entirely different bird, an animal, or a tree on the other. In all designs and their inspirations, a subject's recognition and readability is not so important; the final impact depends on how interestingly space is broken into and composed.

Specific art and craft techniques can be adapted to inspire design in many media. Origami, the Japanese art of paper folding, and other fold-and-dye procedures offer valuable sources for repeat pattern. The types of patterns obtained using these methods depend upon the folding process selected. The number of repeats in the pattern are controlled by the number of folds made. There are three basic folding methods; they all begin by making accordion pleats along the length of the paper. The resulting long strip is then accordion pleated along the folded length in either a square or rectangle fold, a right-angle isosceles triangular fold, or in an equilateral triangular fold. Other factors that may alter the pattern include the number of colors used, which edges are dipped in dye, how they are dipped, and whether the paper is wet or dry. Wet paper produces soft bleeding areas of color that overlap adjoining areas, creating color transparencies. (Where yellow overlaps blue, green results.) Dry paper produces hard, sharp, well-defined edges.

Patterns developed by these methods may be duplicated faithfully on a ceramic bowl as a silk-screened fabric or wallcovering. They may provide a nucleus for further development as an acrylic painting, a modular construction, or jewelry links. A section, such as a half or a quarter of the total dyed piece, could be used in its true scale or blown up or reduced.

The first step of stage one begins with two vertical, slightly bowed lines which touch the bottom and top edges of the format. If lines do not touch the edges of a shape, they "float" and do not create the means necessary for outlining and defining shape. By adding a balancing horizontal line, the space has been fundamentally divided into six spaces. The addition of the third line repeats both directions and also repeats the same angle that occurs when the verticals and horizontal cross. Observe how the addition of only these four lines create eleven shapes with asymmetrical proportions. The progressive four stages indicate the development of a design within a given rectangular format. Each addition to the series becomes successively more complex and could stand alone as an interesting design. Additional lines break up the same space more completely, creating smaller scaled units with more intricate and defined detail.

Four line drawings illustrate how one drawing can retain its identity, yet differ drastically. The first is a simple, uniform, fine-line pen drawing. The lines of the second, drawn with a wider nib than the first, are sketchy and heavier. Linear textural shapes of darker value have been built up via the sketchy technique. The third drawing is made with bold brush strokes. Textural dark-value areas are built up with repeated brush imprints. The fourth, made with various-sized pen points, is the most varied and interesting. The value relationships are dynamically asymmetrical, with the strong white shape on the right cutting into the dark cross-hatched shape. (Note that this shape has not been outlined.) Each texture, with variation, has been repeated within the design. Differences in interval spacing provide the change in values. Small scale, additional detail, and subtlety create further visual interest.

Cutting rectangles from overlaid different colors of transparent tissue paper is another excellent approach to design and color relationships. Balancing and repeating the shapes in each layer must be carefully considered. Begin with a piece of white illustration board and cut rectangles from a first layer of yellow transparent tissue. Add a second layer of red tissue and cut away some rectangles so that some white shows through and some yellow shows through; where the red and yellow are overlaid, orange results. A third blue layer was added with rectangles cut away still exposing some white, some yellow, and some orange. With the combination of blue over red and yellow, the remaining areas appear brown. Cutting away different portions of each color yields interesting design. It is also a marvelous exercise in color mixing as it works with tissues and is an excellent technique for preplanning designs in resist and printing techniques such as batik, silk screening, and others.

Orange Transparency. Bill Hinz. Design built up of various layers of colored tissues. Every overlapping color creates an additional color. The color changes show up as value changes in this black-and-white photograph.

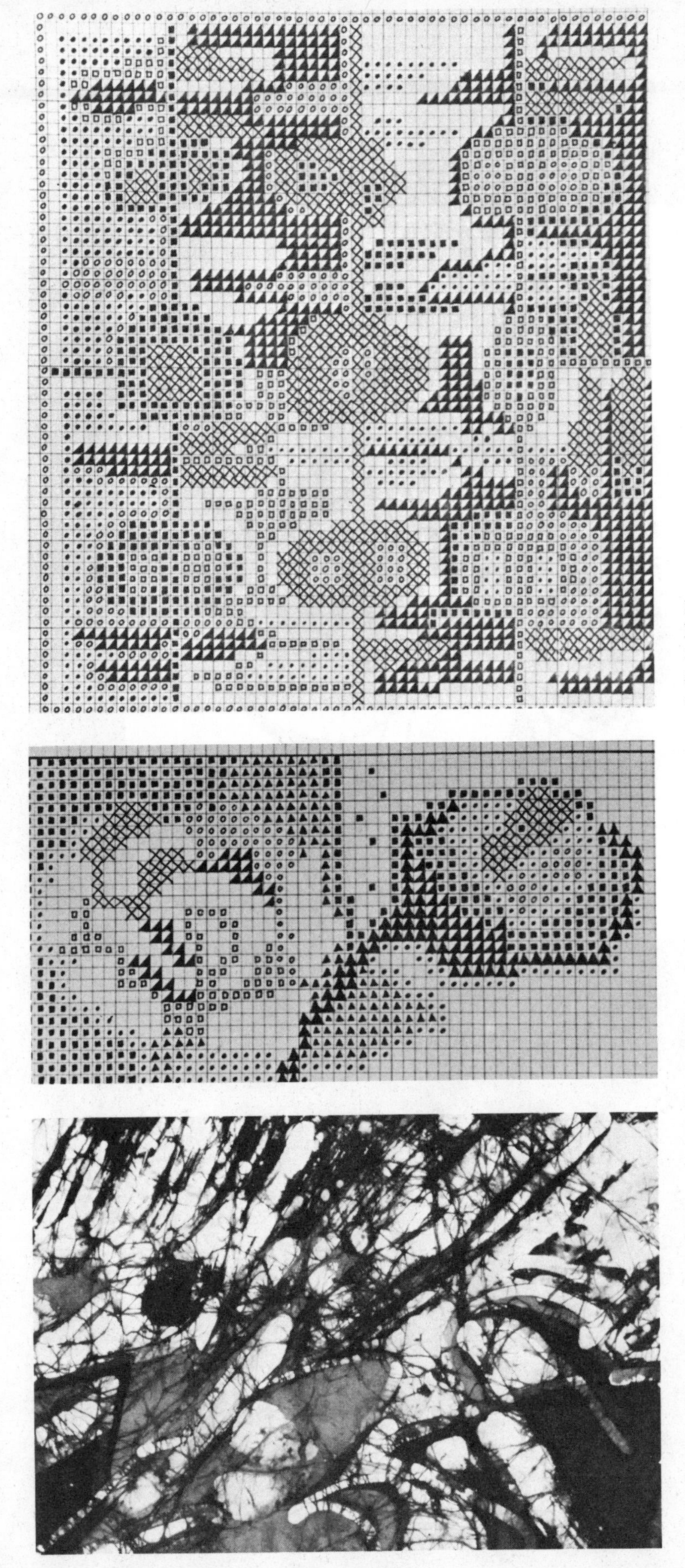

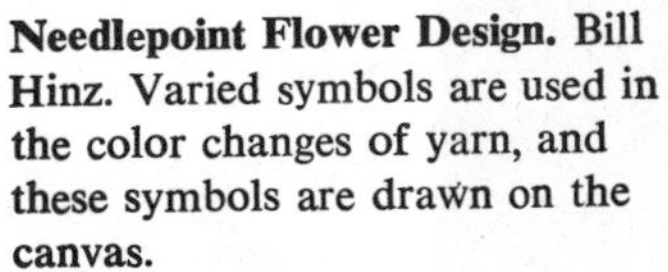

Needlepoint Flower Design. Bill Hinz. Varied symbols are used in the color changes of yarn, and these symbols are drawn on the canvas.

Needlepoint Contemporary Rose Pattern. (Design development) Bill Hinz.

The detail only from a batik could be a design inspiration for needlepoint and would be worked out on the canvas in symbols, as above. Judith Irany.

Bimorphic Bird-Plant. (Opposite) Jay Hinz. Sketchbook drawing. Ink. Keeping a sketchbook of ideas will give you an immediate available source for design inspiration.

Piano Keyboard. Bill Hinz. Pencil rendering for a hooked wool wall hanging, using tissue overlays of different values.

Piano Keyboard, Face and Bottle. Bill Hinz. Colored-pencil rendering for a hooked wool wall hanging.

Musician. Bill Hinz. Colored-pencil rendering for a hooked wool wall hanging.

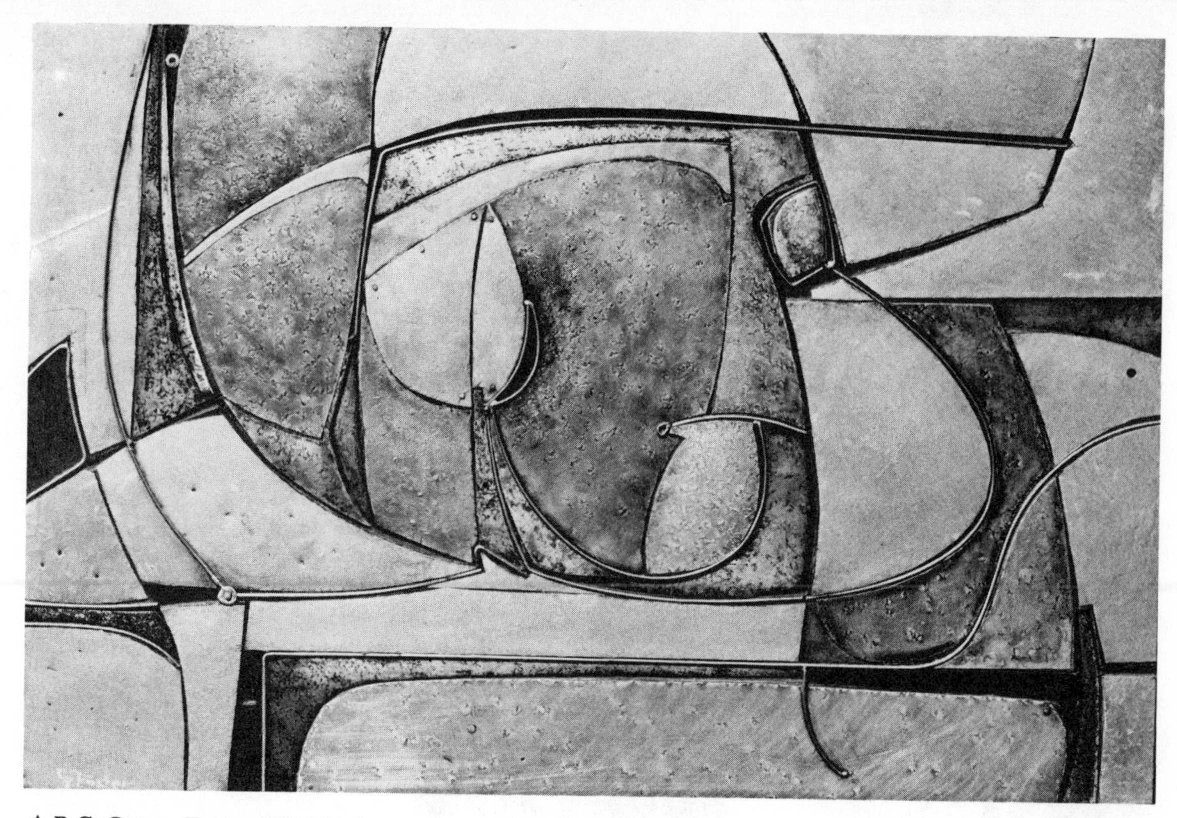

A B C. George Foster. 17½″ high, 26″ wide. Metal collage. Shape, line, value, texture, and dot interpreted in different metals from soft-drink cans. Photographed at Collectors' Showroom, Chicago

A Journey. Berni Gorski. 24″ wide, 16″ high. Black, gray, and ocher batik on cotton broadcloth mounted on natural raw silk mat. Courtesy, artist. Collection, Dr. and Mrs. Daniel Kline, Cincinnati, Ohio

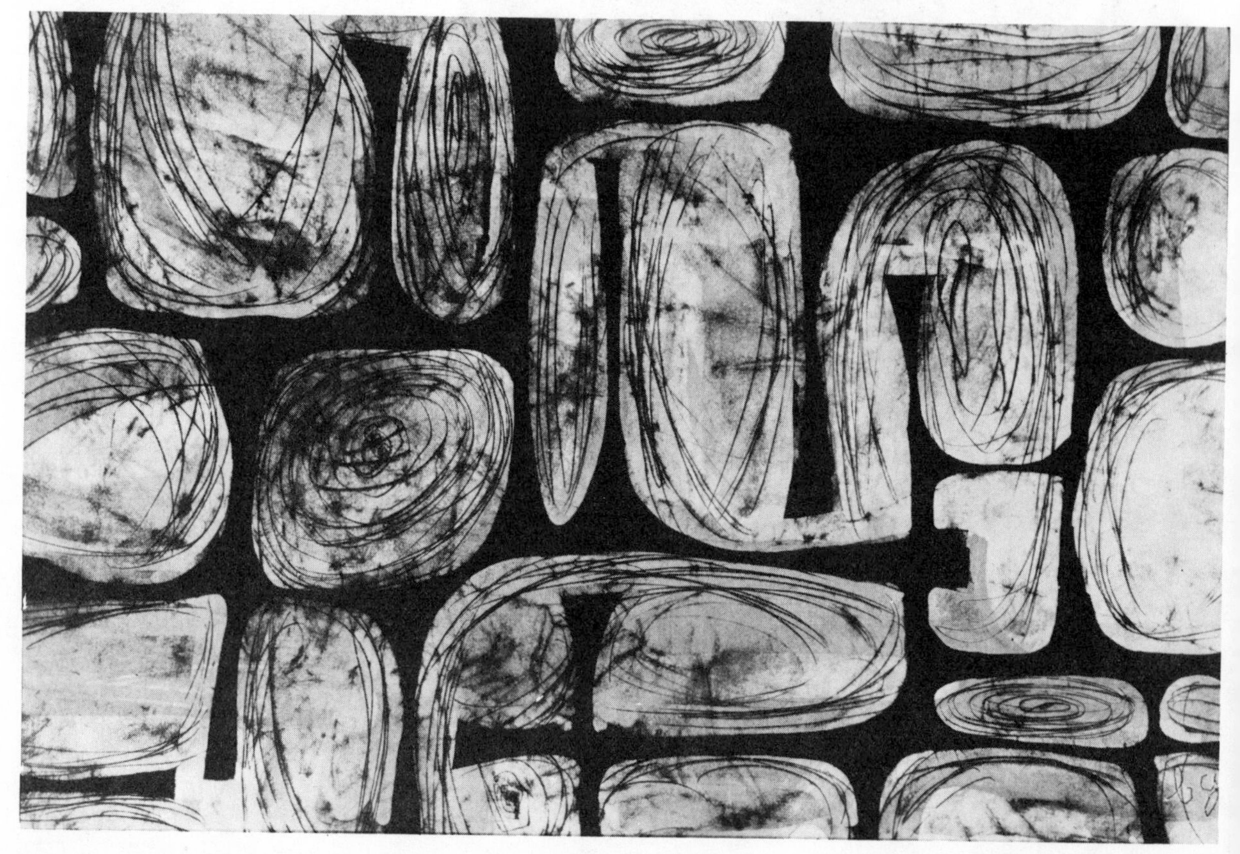

EXERCISES

1 Make a starch print. (See page 199 for formula.)
   A. Select the most interesting section of the print.
   B. Interpret this section into lines, shapes, and values.
   C. Interpret the value design into colors of the same value.
2 Fold several squares of paper towel in different ways. Dip the corners and/or edges into various colors of food coloring. Select one of these patterns and interpret it into a design, duplicating the colors and transparencies of the original fold-and-dye piece.
3 Create a design having shape and value in five stages. Be certain that at each stage the design balances.
4 Create a line design. Reproduce it three times, using different types of lines each time to change the character of the design.
5 Create two separate design units to work together as one unit. Make the units capable of joining top to bottom and side to side.

SELECTED BIBLIOGRAPHY

Anderson, Donald M., *Elements of Design.* New York, Holt, Rinehart & Winston, Inc., 1961.

Arnheim, Rudolf, *Art and Visual Perception: A Psychology of the Creative Eye.* Berkeley and Los Angeles, University of California Press, 1966.

Ballinger, Louise Bowen, and Vroman, Thomas F., *Design Sources and Resources.* New York, Reinhold Publishing Corp., 1965.

Bevlin, Marjorie Elliott, *Design Through Discovery.* New York, Holt, Rinehart & Winston, Inc., 1970.

Bothwell, Dorr, and Frey, Marlys, *Notan: The Dark-Light Principle of Design.* New York, Van Nostrand-Reinhold Co., 1968.

Collier, Graham, *Form, Space, and Vision.* Englewood Cliffs, N.J., Prentice-Hall, Inc., 1965.

Gardner, Helen, *Art Through the Ages,* 5th ed. New York, Harcourt, Brace & Co., 1970.

Garrett, Lillian, *Visual Design: A Problem-Solving Approach.* New York, Reinhold Publishing Corp., 1967.

Hastie, Reid, and Schmidt, Christian, *Encounter with Art.* New York, McGraw-Hill Book Co.

Hickethier, Alfred, *Color Mixing by Numbers.* New York, Reinhold Publishing Corp., 1963.

Hollander, Annette, *Decorative Papers and Fabrics.* New York, Van Nostrand-Reinhold Co., 1971.

Jacobson, Egbert, *Basic Color.* Chicago, Paul Theobald, 1948.

Kranz, Stewart, and Fisher, Robert, *The Design Continuum; an Approach to Understanding Visual Forms.* New York, Reinhold Publishing Corp., 1966.

Meilach, Dona Z., *Contemporary Batik and Tie-Dye.* New York, Crown Publishing Co., 1973.

———, *Macramé, Creative Design in Knotting.* New York, Crown Publishing Co., 1971.

Meilach, Dona Z., and Seiden, Donald M., *Direct Metal Sculpture.* New York, Crown Publishing Co., 1966.

Meilach, Dona Z., and Snow, Lee Erlin, Chicago, *Creative Stitchery.* Henry Regnery Co., 1970.

———, *Weaving Off Loom.* Chicago, Henry Regnery Co., 1973.

Moholy-Nagy, L., *Vision In Motion.* Chicago, Paul Theobald, 1947.

Miles, Walter, *Designs For Craftsmen.* Garden City, New York, Doubleday & Co., Inc., 1962.

Proctor, Richard M., *The Principles of Pattern for Craftsmen and Designers.* New York, Van Nostrand-Reinhold Co., 1969.

Röttger, Ernst, and Klante, Deiter, *Creative Drawing Point and Line.* New York, Reinhold Publishing Corp., 1963.

———, ———, and Salzmann, Friedrich, *Surfaces in Creative Drawing.* New York, Van Nostrand-Reinhold Co., 1969.

de Sausmarez, Maurice, *Basic Design: The Dynamics of Visual Form.* New York, Reinhold Publishing Corp., 1964.

Scott, Robert Gillam, *Design Fundamentals.* New York, McGraw-Hill Book Co., Inc., 1951.

Sneum, Gunnar, *Teaching Design and Form.* New York, Reinhold Publishing Corp., 1965.

INDEX